The Widc

Timothy E. Tyre   8/2018

To Jack & Mary
I'm so pleased to
hear you enjoyed the
"Widowmaker". Although
my Mom recently passed,
Dad is still young at
94!
Warmest
Tim

Timothy E.Tyre

Copyright © 2016 Timothy Tyre

ISBN: 1537612913
ISBN-13: 978-1537612911

DEDICATION

To Marilyn, my loving wife, who is patient and quietly encouraging. Without her support, aviation training, military service, the family and all the other stuff would not have happened. Thank you especially for the loving care of my parents.

To my children and grandchildren, this book is your heritage. It speaks to the selflessness of the greatest generation and to the power of love in a relationship which has endured over 70 years.

CONTENTS

The Widowmaker

ACKNOWLEDGMENTS

This book simply would not have happened without the meticulous and loving attention given to the editing process, graphics, and photo preparation by my daughter Kateri Tyre, Graham Blankenbaker, and my dear friend professor George Sargent. Already a published author, Kateri has enormous artistic skill, a remarkable capacity for attention to detail, and a huge work ethic. Graham is equally talented, and like my dad, he admirably elects to draw little attention to himself. George is a retired professor emeritus from the University of Wisconsin - Whitewater. He encouraged completion of this work in a selfless and kind way. Their work during the final stages of the book is deeply appreciated.

Tim

PROLOGUE

The B-26 combat crew was aboard and ready while 2nd Lt. Eddie Tyre began the pre-flight checklists. The early morning mission briefing had been completed and the flight of 12 Marauders were going through the complex lists required to get underway. The flight's crew chief knelt in the cockpit next to Lt. Tyre and reviewed the "ready for flight" list. Lt. Tyre signed the document certifying that the pilot of the mission accepted the aircraft as ready for combat flight. The number #1 engine start procedure was begun and the crew chief, who was now on the ground with a large fire extinguisher available, gave a ready sign. The propeller was cycled and Lt. Tyre pushed the start button. The powerful Pratt-Whitney, R-2800 Double Wasp radial engine roared to life. A "thunderous and deafening" sound was heard as the 1,850 horsepower, 18 cylinder engine came alive. The 19 year old

Eddie Tyre in flight suit

pilot adjusted the throttle to a steady 1200 rpm and readied the #2 engine for the same start sequence. Once both engines were synchronized, a single, powerful "humming" sound was achieved and the warbird was ready for taxi. No tower communications occurred to authorize taxi, as radio silence was required in this war time situation. Lt. Tyre gave a thumbs up for the crew chief to pull the wheel chocks and the #36 combat mission was underway. A flight of 12 Marauders was readying for take-off and formation for the approximate 2 hour route to southern Germany. The intelligence officers had warned that heavy FLAK would begin about 30 minutes into the flight when the bombers crossed the Rhine and Germany began to fight back.

Taxiing into position the aircraft engines were "run-up" to allow a final check by stressing the engines to near full power. Back to engine idle, and the fuel tanks were topped off with gasoline to support the long flight to and from the target. The squadron commander was easy to spot, as he stood in the rear of his jeep and waved a checkered flag every 30 seconds to launch another Marauder. With full military power, the B-26 seemed to catapult down the runway, with a bomb load and all machine guns ready.

B-26 on take-off

Lt. Tyre watched the airspeed indicator and waited for the 125 mph "rotation speed" to pull back on the control yoke and get the heavy war machine into the air. Gear up lights followed, and the Marauder responded with more speed with the drag of the gear gone. The next step required each flight of 3 aircraft to form up in a "V" with the lead plane at center. Immediately behind was the second, third and fourth waves. At a cruising altitude of 6,000' the formation tightened and Lt. Tyre brought his ship 10 feet behind the first wave and slightly above. The engines and propellers were adjusted for cruise with manifold pressure (engine power) settings and 2200 rpm for the adjustable propellers. The aircraft formation was heading due north into Germany traveling at a leisurely 190 mph.

At 0830 hours, just as briefed by the intelligence Officer, FLAK began. The smooth ride for the formation ceased, as FLAK bursts rocked the planes. Lt. Tyre said silent prayers that the FLAK bursts stayed above and not below the bombers, as the white hot shrapnel bursts would explode upwards, to rip through the thin aluminum skin of the warplanes. In what seemed like hours later, the raiders were

B-26 bombs-away on target

suddenly only 3 minutes from the target and they increased power to a full 236 mph with wings and altitude held to an exact standard. As the bombardier lined up the target, the final 20 seconds before bombs away made the world seem almost in slow motion as the young, tense but much focused pilot and combat crew waited for the bombardier to "toggle" the bomb load. The plane climbed a bit with the sudden release of hundreds of pounds of bomb weight and then Lt. Eddie Tyre began the required, immediate, steep bank angle to a 45 degree diving left turn. The Marauders turned away from the targets and raced for home. Combat mission number #36 was half done. *What will happen to us on the way back to Dijon? thought Lt. Tyre ...*

1 PROVISO HIGH SCHOOL AND THE WORLD

December 7th, 1939
Proviso High School, Maywood, Illinois
8:15AM, Homeroom Class, Mr. Goodwin, Science

In a class of 28 students, Shirley Litton stood out for her contagious enthusiasm for school. With thick, reddish-brown locks and a personality that exceeded her 5'1" frame, she was an academic standout, easily winning medals for scholarship and earning a place on the National Honor Society. The winsome young high school student, nicknamed "Scottie" by her friends and family, was never idle. Outside of her studies, she found time for theater, girls' basketball, the school newspaper, and a part-time job as a library page at the Elmwood Park Public Library.

Shirley enjoyed her library science and botany classes. Her botany instructor, Mr. Goodwin, endeared himself to Shirley and the rest of the students with his fatherly ways. Every lecture began with, "Where did we leave off yesterday?" His classroom was often full with wide eyed students on those chilly December mornings. Some were calling it an early winter that year.

Proviso High School Years

The Litton family lived in the Chicago suburb of Elmwood Park, a quiet, middle-class community. The great depression was almost over but many still looked for work and struggled to afford mortgage payments. Neighbors whispered about a real estate practice that promised to help local home owners by selling secondary bank notes, but the contractual fine print required no sales to Americans of Jewish faith or descent. To Shirley's father, Park Litton, this practice was a sample of the "bad things out there in the world" and it hinted at the dark events brewing in the German Republic.

The only pre-war news that Proviso High School students received at the time was in the theater. "Movietone News" trailers highlighted current events and occasionally mentioned the rise of Nazism and German and Japanese hegemony. Shirley's father, a former Army Doughboy in World War I, made every effort to protect his beloved Scottie from such ugly things developing in the world at the time. As a result, she was only minimally aware of the growing evil across the Atlantic.

Shirley first met Eddie Tyre, a modest and quiet young man, in her freshman year at Proviso High. Eddie was allegedly struggling in English class with his coursework, and Shirley was surprised to have him "on my shoulder." (Many years later, at 90 years of age and after 68 years of marriage, he admitted with a grin, "it might have been a technique.")

Although described by others as shy, Eddie was twice elected as the President of Hi-Y, a non-sectarian fellowship based on the four-fold creed of "Clean Speech, Clean Sports, Clean Scholarship, and Clean Living." His small group of friends was studious and serious; one of his closest friends, Dick Carnwright later attended the U.S. Military Academy at West Point and achieved the rank of full Colonel in the Air Force. Eddie was active in sports and band during high school. He played basketball and baseball, and also played clarinet in the marching band. The Proviso High marching band won national attention at the time by being the first to wear self-contained, battery-powered lights during performances.

Eddie began his days at school that year in Miss West's U.S. history class. "I think I got good grades in her class because I actually paid attention." He rounded out his industrial arts curriculum with classes in architectural drawing, machining, and woodworking.

Eddie's father, also named Edward, was Vice President of an office furniture company in Chicago. He settled with his three sons and his wife, Pearl, in Maywood, Illinois, the largest village in Proviso Township. Eddie, the oldest of the three boys, took after his mother, herself a professional ice skater with natural athletic abilities in many sports.

The Depression came early to Maywood and the Tyre family was no exception. They lost their first home in 1931, but despite this early financial setback, the family always had meals to eat and a car to drive. Eddie purchased his first car, a 1923 Ford Model A convertible, when he was 17 years old. This somewhat flashy, black vehicle lasted only two weeks; the gears and transmission were bad, and "it would not back up." He sold the car several weeks later for the same $25 purchase price he purchased it for.

During high school, Eddie did not feel personally connected to the war. Although he was aware of the War Department torpedo factory in nearby Forest Park, Illinois, he did not feel especially bothered by this or the events in Europe. Eddie occasionally got into innocent mischief, playing Halloween pranks, drawing on the neighbors' windows with bees-wax, and sneaking out to see his friends. Although he never admitted getting into any trouble, Eddie flashed a proud little grin as he told of quietly creeping in after-hours at the family cottage.

Shirley's younger brother Jack was strongly opposed to this sort of behavior and the two would sometimes quarrel. "I had a temper, and I do remember slamming the front door after an argument with my brother and breaking the glass panes... that got me grounded." This passionate, spitfire personality grabbed Eddie's attention.

When Eddie first laid eyes on Shirley, it was love from "the first time I saw her." He thought to himself, "This is someone I need to know... she is like a goddess." Eddie never had serious conversations with a girl before he met Shirley. Classes together were a special treat, and Eddie feigned problems with English coursework to request her help, even though he himself was a silver-medalist academic.

In general, life in Maywood, Illinois was quiet, peaceful, and innocent for the young couple.

December 7th, 1939
German Foreign Ministry
Wilhelmplatz, Berlin, Germany

Growing nationalism in Germany was steadily taking hold, stimulated by Adolf Hitler's passionate speeches and efforts to improve the failing domestic economy. Earlier that year, Hitler had successfully negotiated a non-aggression pact with Russia. Confident the Russians would not interfere, Hitler ordered German tanks to invade Polish territory on September 1st, 1939. Britain and France, standing by their guarantee of Poland's border, declared war on Germany in a radio address delivered by British Prime Minister Neville Chamberlain on September 3rd, 1939.

Hitler was unusually quiet with his aides that day. He expected war weary Britain to swiftly capitulate. Although reluctant to engage in another land war, both Britain and France were determined to slow Hitler's ambitions. Hitler intended to punish the British and simultaneously execute a tactical maneuver to hasten an early surrender. Together with his Air Marshall, Hermann Goering, they planned the London "Blitz", a massive and unrelenting nighttime air offensive. Goering's unprecedented military plan would strike at civilian targets in London. The powerful German Luftwaffe, equipped with both medium and long range lethal bombers, including the Dornier-17 and 217, the Heinkel-111, and the Messerschmitt 109 and110, easily navigated to the London area as fire bombs gave pilots a clear and visible target miles away.

The British suffered tragic losses. In the first year of the Blitz campaign, civilian casualties were estimated at more than 60,000. At the completion of the campaign, over one million Britons were left homeless. Early one morning, after a long night of bombing, newly appointed Prime Minister Winston Churchill walked the streets of London. He was moved to tears as his countrymen stepped out of the rubble, waving the Union Jack and encouraging him to carry-on[1].

The German juggernaut rolled through Europe using the concept of Blitzkrieg, or "lightning war", first tested on the Polish with devastating success. This technique was designed to create psychological shock and disorganize the opposing force. It relied on the use of surprise, speed, and superior firepower.

The attack on Poland began with the STUKA JU 87 dive-bombers used

STUKA dive bombers

as precision ground-attack weapons. These planes led the invasion with rollover techniques from 4,000 feet, creating a wailing sound during their dive configuration. This frightening event was intensified by the cardboard sirens attached to their 1,100-pound bombs, and ultimately became the propaganda symbol of German air power.

Immediately following the Luftwaffe air attacks, the XIX Panzer Corps rolled across the countryside, traveling 140 miles to Warsaw in less than a week. It was a mechanized nightmare for the citizens of Poland. The Poles, the French, the British, and their Commonwealth partners were stunned as the Wehrmacht used this strategy to successfully invade both France and the Low Countries of Europe through the spring of 1940. The world far away from Shirley and Eddie was becoming increasingly deadly[2].

December 7th, 1939
Tokyo, Japan

Fearful of Russian expansionism and emboldened with a sense of empire, the Japanese invaded Manchuria in 1931, creating the puppet state of Manchukuo. In December of 1936, previously warring factions of China suspended their civil war and established the Second United Front to resist further invasion by the Japanese.

Responding to this event, Japan unleashed the full extent of its military ambitions. Through a short year in 1937, the Japanese army captured the Chinese cities of Peking, Tientsin, and Shanghai, demonstrating clear designs on the capital city of Nanking. The shocking events during the "Rape of Nanking" were notable for crimes against humanity as the Japanese raped, murdered, and looted without mercy. By late 1938, the port cities of Hankow and Canton also succumbed to the Japanese.

In the year that followed, and motivated by these successes, Imperial Japanese Navy Commander Minoru Genda[3] developed an elaborate and daring plan. The Japanese would launch a surprise attack on the U.S. Navy base at Pearl Harbor. Later, following evidence of undeniable success for the mission, Admiral Yamamoto was credited with penning this *waka* ("Japanese poetry"):

> *I fear all we have done*
> *Is to awaken a sleeping giant*
> *And fill him with a terrible resolve*[4]

Photographs this section courtesy of: (a) National Museum of USAF, (b) National Archives, (c) Tyre family archives

---

1 The Blitzkrieg is discussed in great detail in Winston Churchill's "Grand Alliance" (1950)

2 Smith, Peter C. The Junkers JU867 Stuka.

3 Peattie, Mark R. Naval Institute Press (2001)

4 Agawa, H. (1979)

2 A RELATIONSHIP GROWS

December 7th, 1940
Elmwood Park, Illinois

A year later, Eddie and Shirley had begun their courtship. Eddie regularly saved his 50 cents per hour wages as a part-time grocery store stock boy to afford dates with Shirley. Typically, their dates began with Eddie's short ride on the streetcar, followed by a ride on the west town bus through Forest Park. The combined fare was 10 cents. He got off the bus at the picturesque roundabout in Elmwood Park and walked the four blocks to Westwood at 7770 Elm Grove Drive. Nearby stood the Lutheran church, a stately and beautiful red brick edifice, where several of Shirley's childhood friends later married. Shirley's home was situated on a narrow road, and built from distinctively soft yellow solid brick, with a front porch that allowed casual sitting and conversation during the summer months.

Eddie usually dressed casually, with tan corduroy pants and a matching sweater. He took care to comb his hair neatly but encountered no problems with shaving. (He began shaving at age 22, after leaving the Army Air Corps.) Shirley typically wore plaid skirts, with the white collar of her shirt showing at the neck of her sweater. Eddie was captivated by her beauty and articulate speech; indeed, her tendency to correct his speech persists to this day. Their weekly dates usually consisted of a theater show and then Eddie would take Shirley to a restaurant for 20-cent chocolate sodas. They both enjoyed films staring Shirley Temple, who consistently delighted the audience with tap dance and singing routines. Eddie was careful to catch the last bus home. If he missed it, the long walk to Maywood was over 7 miles in the dark, through the undeveloped countryside, with little chance of thumbing a ride. Unfortunately, he had to endure this worrisome "long dark walk" at least twice.

The young couple loved to attend football games at Proviso High School, where Shirley would sit with the girlfriends of other marching band members and listen to Eddie play his clarinet. The keen rivalry between wealthy Oak Park High and the less affluent Proviso students ensured that band competitions were spirited events, and Mr. Tallmadge's Proviso High band used special lights on their musical instruments to delight the crowd. After the games, Shirley and Eddie would often join other couples on double dates and visit The Huddle, a popular soda shop. Many of these friends stayed in close contact throughout the war years that were just around the corner.

Occasionally, they visited the graves of Shirley's paternal grandparents, Roland Noble Litton and Elizabeth Litton. Growing up, Shirley always felt that her grandparents were a "letter away," having settled in Los Angeles, California. Both Irish and English by descent, they insisted on academic pursuits for their grandchildren, especially reading. Roland was rather distant from Shirley, especially in comparison to her maternal grandfather, Jock, a fun-loving, street musician from Edinburgh, Scotland. He encouraged Shirley to enjoy music and dancing. Shirley's mother Marguerite exemplified the family's love of music. She was a self-taught pianist who played by ear and would frequently accompany Shirley when she danced on the dining room table as a young child. Both of her maternal grandparents had a thick Scottish brogue, noticeable in song and speech, but Shirley's diction was always precise, due in part to her Grandmother Elizabeth's insistence on proper English.

Summer 1940
Petit Lake, Illinois

The Sea Maid was a beautiful, varnished, cedar boat with four seats, windshield, and a powerful 55-horsepower Chris-Craft outboard engine. Eddie and his two younger brothers, Bob and Tom, loved to drive fast on the small Petit Lake area where the Tyre family vacationed. Waterskiing on the surf-board-like apparatus took skill and an element of recklessness. Eddie liked the sense of freedom the boat gave him throughout the interconnected chain of lakes region in northern Illinois.

As fate would have it, the couple was completely unaware of their coincidental plans for summer vacation on the pretty little lake. Late one afternoon, Shirley was sitting near the water, relaxing and enjoying the beautiful views of Petit Lake, where her parents rented a small cottage for the summer. She noticed the curious wooden speedboat that kept racing back and forth just off the pier. The boat slowed and idled towards her. At the helm was Eddie Tyre, who casually remarked, "I live here in the summer. My parents own a cottage across the lake."

From then on, Eddie and Shirley enjoyed summer days together exploring the lakes and many canals that connected them in *The*

11

Sea Maid. Returning late in the evening one night, they were greeted by Shirley's father at the end of the pier, who made it very clear that "respectable hours" were required when his Scottie was out. Eddie nervously apologized. "He definitely got my attention" Eddie recalled.

As their courtship continued throughout the year, Eddie began to notice Shirley's devotion to Sunday mass at St. Celestine's Catholic Church in Elmwood Park. Eddie felt impressed by her religious commitment and discipline. His Christian Scientist family had a more casual approach to religion. On Sundays, Eddie's dad would "head the car to the local salvage yard instead of church" to look for unusual items to bring home. Edward Tyre Senior was a quiet but interesting man, forever tinkering with gadgets and inventing things. Shirley soon inspired Eddie to accompany her to church on Sundays. "I did it for her," he remarked.

By fall, the couple was dating with such regularity that on Eddie's arrival to Shirley's home her father would usually remark in humorous fashion, "It's him again." With the prospect of war looming larger, the U.S. government introduced rationing across the country, and the couple's mothers swapped knowledge of special food sales to offset the hardship.

By the end of 1940, though military service still seemed unlikely, Eddie felt that the difficulties in Europe were uncomfortably close to home. War bond sales in the U.S. were increasing, as were reports of Hitler's aggression in Europe. Popular sentiment at the time was that troubles in Europe would be short lived, and the U.S. role limited to manufacturing war supplies for the British. Having heard her father's concerns about President Roosevelt's support of the British, Shirley was a bit more cynical. Park Litton feared that the President's policies were slowly drawing the United States into the conflict.

3 A DAY TO REMEMBER

December 7th, 1941
Pearl Harbor, Hawaii

A total of six Imperial Japanese Navy aircraft carriers of the battle group Kido Butai (Hawaii Strike Force) turned into the wind about 250 nautical miles north of Oahu. The first wave of attack planes started their engines in the pre-dawn light. All 182 of the fighters and bombers in the first wave gathered in the air and followed the signaling lights of the lead plane. The surprise attack on Pearl Harbor was underway.

At 7:53 am, the first bombs fell on an unsuspecting fleet of ninety-six U.S. warships closely anchored in the harbor. The first wave of bomber attacks triggered a barrage of panicked and disorganized radio messages, "AIR RAID ON PEARL HARBOR! THIS IS NO DRILL!"

An armor-piercing bomb struck the forward magazine of the USS Arizona and the resulting explosions crippled the warship. The USS Oklahoma took three torpedo hits almost immediately after the first Japanese bombs fell. As she began to capsize, two more torpedoes struck home, trapping many of the crew inside.

Four hundred and twenty-nine of her officers and enlisted men were killed or missing.

The unexpected Japanese attack delivered monumental damage to the U.S. fleet at Pearl Harbor. In total, twenty-one warships were sunk or seriously damaged. The battleships USS Arizona, USS Oklahoma and USS Utah were completely destroyed. Six other battleships -- the USS Tennessee, USS Nevada, USS Maryland, USS Pennsylvania, USS West Virginia, and USS California -- were severely damaged but eventually returned to service. 188 U.S. aircraft were destroyed; 2,403 Americans were killed and 1,178 others were wounded[5].

USS Arizona and USS Oklahoma before the bombing (above)
December 7th, 1941 Japanese attack on Pearl Harbor (below)

Although damage to the U.S. fleet was significant, the real impact of the Japanese attack was to awaken the American public. Prior to Pearl Harbor, isolationist policies held sway throughout the country, especially in the Chicago area. Now, the "sleeping giant," as many called America at that time, was profoundly outraged. The following day, the United States formally declared war on Japan. Shirley and Eddie's lives would soon change forever.

December 7th, 1941
Imperial Palace
Tokyo, Japan

It was mid-afternoon when Japanese Foreign Minister Shigenori Togo informed the Emperor of the initial success of the surprise attack at Pearl Harbor in Hawaii. The next day, December 8th, the Japanese Broadcasting Corporation announced by radio to the Japanese citizens:

> *We now present you urgent news. The Army and Navy Divisions of Imperial General Headquarters jointly announced at six o'clock this morning, December 8th, that the Imperial Army and Navy forces have begun hostilities against American and British forces in the Pacific at dawn today.*[6]

December 7th, 1941
Berlin, Germany

Germany enthusiastically responded to news of the carefully organized Japanese attacks. Hitler was now convinced the war would be won by the combined strength of a Japanese and German war machine. Well aware of Japan's remarkably long history of military successes, Hitler arranged to have a medal presented to Japanese Foreign Minister Hiroshi Oshima to honor the occasion of this alliance. On December 14th, 1941, during the ceremony to present the Grand Cross of

Japanese Foreign Minister Oshima wears his medal.

The Grand Cross of the Distinguished Order of the German Eagle

the Distinguished Order of the German Eagle, Hitler complimented the Japanese use of a sneak attack "as the best way to start a war."

The Japanese attack dissolved internal German conflict over how to deal with the Americans, who had declared neutrality but were secretly supplying the British. The German U-boat commanders in the North Atlantic were vexed with orders that disallowed firing on neutral ships. Historical reviews of the war would later establish that if the Americans had not continued sending supplies to the British, Churchill and his countrymen would likely not have survived the German campaign.

December 7th, 1941
10 Downing Street
London, England

Immediately upon learning of the Japanese attacks, Churchill issued a declaration of war against Japan. World War on a global basis was now underway. Italy had already joined the Axis powers and most of Europe had fallen. Now, the Japanese were attacking British colonies and allies throughout the Pacific. To make matters worse, the British had recently suffered successive defeats at the hands of German forces, from Dunkirk in France, to North Africa. Even the deep-water perimeter surrounding the British Isles had not stopped the mighty German Luftwaffe raids on London and its citizens. The island of Great Britain stood alone, separated only by the narrow English Channel.

Winston Churchill victory sign

With the U.S. officially joining the war, the embattled British were at once relieved and also grimly aware of the daunting tasks ahead. Although the American manufacturing engine was sure to be a major factor, Churchill was very well aware that the United States was not ready for modern warfare and would likely require a year or more to prepare. He contacted President Roosevelt and pledged complete support. The history texts quote him as saying, "God be with you[7]."

December 7th, 1941
7770 Elmgrove Drive
Elmwood Park, Illinois

Newsboys flooded the usually quiet streets of Elmwood Park, wild eyed and shouting, "Extra! Extra! Read all about the attack on the U.S. Navy at Pearl Harbor!" Radio announcements reported a litany of terrifying details to the American public throughout the day. Reeling from the shock, Shirley's family gathered later that evening for dinner and discussion with close friends, some of whom were World War I veterans. Hoping to lift the atmosphere in the room, Shirley's mother Marguerite played patriotic songs on the piano. As passions in the room swelled, one of the veterans proudly shouted, "We should go enlist!" Park, who was partially deaf from combat explosions from the First World War responded, "What?" Shirley couldn't help but laugh with a little relief, knowing that his age and hearing loss would prevent him from re-enlisting.

Eddie was in the Lido Theater in Maywood when news about Pearl Harbor flashed across the screen. Sitting with his good friends, Dick Carnwright and Hugh Galston, the three boys were all stunned. Later, at home, Eddie could feel his father's thinly veiled outrage. As a former Navy bi-plane aerial gunner, Edward Tyre senior knew what these troubling events likely meant for his son and the rest of the country.

The following day, Monday, December 8th, Proviso High School administrators instructed the students to assemble in their homeroom classes for an announcement. President Roosevelt addressed a joint session of Congress and, via radio, the entire nation:

Yesterday, on December 7, 1941, a date which will live in infamy, the United States was suddenly and deliberately attacked by naval and air forces of the Empire of Japan.

Shirley listened to the President's declaration and anxiously anticipated what it might mean for Eddie. In response to the address, Congress immediately passed a formal declaration:

That the state of war between the United States and the Imperial Government of Japan which has thus been thrust upon the United States is hereby formally declared, and the President is hereby authorized and directed to employ the entire naval and military forces of the United States and the resources of the Government to carry on war against the Imperial

Roosevelt signing declaration of war

Government of Japan, and to bring the conflict to a successful termination, all the resources of the country are hereby pledged by the Congress of the United States.

The remainder of the school year at Proviso High felt different for the students. Eddie knew "this would directly affect me now." Friends began to enlist in the military even before graduating in the spring ceremony. Despite the serious events

Students at Proviso High School organize to sell defense stamps, 1942.

that overshadowed daily life, the student body fought to maintain a sense of normalcy, holding fundraisers to support the victims of the Pearl Harbor attack.

The couple attended senior prom together, Eddie wearing a formal tuxedo and Shirley, by his account, in a "very beautiful blue dress." This year, the prom was held in Oak Park, considered "enemy territory" for the Proviso High football team and band members. During the grand march at the beginning of the festivities, all of the students locked arms together before the dancing began.

As a senior, plans for college study were steadily on Shirley's mind throughout spring semester, 1942. Rosary College in nearby Lake Forest Illinois, a pre-eminent institution for the study of library science, naturally made the top of her list. She

visited the stately campus with her parents and was awe-struck by the beauty of its ivy-covered, neo-Gothic architecture. At the encouragement of her parents, Shirley applied for and was granted a full scholarship based on her record of academic excellence.

In the fall, Shirley enthusiastically began her studies at Rosary College. The school was run by the Dominican Teaching Sisters, a Roman Catholic group admired for an insistence upon scholarship and proper conduct by the young women in their charge. Sister Mary Aurelia, president of the college, exemplified these values. On the occasion of being called to her office, a student was expected to knock respectfully on the large wooden door, wait for an invitation to enter, and stand at attention for the duration of the meeting. Upon leaving the office, a student was expected to gracefully back out of the room, never turning her back to Sister Aurelia.

Photographs this section courtesy of: (a) National Museum of USAF, (b) National Archives, (c) Tyre family archives

---

5 Read an excellent summary of US losses in Zimm, Alan D. (2011)

6 Weintraub, Stanley, Long Day's Journey into War, Lyons Press, 1991

7 "The Grand Alliance", Winston Churchill (1950)

4 AVIATION ASPIRATIONS

Summer 1942
Maywood, Illinois

After graduation from Proviso High School, Eddie began working in the mailroom at the HOL Corporation in the massive Merchandise Mart in downtown Chicago. Military service was looming for all young men his age, and "to not go into service was considered a disgrace." Rather than wait to be drafted, Eddie considered more immediate options for enlistment. The recruiting posters depicting Army Air Corps aviators were alluring and, according to Eddie, "everybody wanted to be a pilot." Aside from Eddie's own father, the only other aviator he knew of was his next-door neighbor, Charles Lindbergh,

famous for his solo, non-stop flight across the Atlantic. At the time, Lindbergh was flying for the U.S. Mail service, using a grass airstrip located approximately 6 blocks away on the grounds of the Hines Veteran's Hospital.

As Eddie contemplated his options, so too did Shirley. Eddie had a competitor for Shirley's attention. Another graduate of Proviso High School and several years older, David Hogan was known to be quite articulate and skilled in English. He had already enlisted in the U.S. Navy and was preparing for deployments in the Atlantic theater of operations. Shirley frequently received letters from him filled with lavish poetry and insistent declarations of his plans to marry her. David dreamed of them together as a couple, in a post-war world where Shirley enjoyed an "idyllic University life," while David taught English studies. U.S. Navy Ensign Hogan wrote to her in 1943:

My very lovely Princess
Smith Hall
September 21, 1943

Sweetheart... I've done a heap of thinking. Mostly that I am so much in love with you. Your letter, which scolded for being so lonesome, was very nice because you call me dear every now and then. I like that a lot!! Oh Princess, I've told you in every way that I could, I love you an awful lot. I don't really have to write how I feel about everything ... I'm sure you know.

I've been miserable lately because I want you to love me. If you don't love me a little now, what chance will I have later? When I think of someone other than myself dating you, I grit my teeth and I know if I ever catch up with that fellow, I swear I'll tear him apart and break every bone in his body!!

With all my love and hope,   David

Photographs this section courtesy of: (a) National Museum of USAF,
(b) National Archives, (c) Tyre family archives

---

5 FLIGHT TRAINING

Spring 1943
North West Texas

Eddie headed for basic training at Sheppard Field in northern Texas in March of 1943. Shirley accompanied him to the train depot in Chicago, along with Eddie's parents, Pearl and Edward. "They were all proud of me, I remember that for sure." On arrival at Sheppard Field, the young Army Air Corps cadets were subjected to especially stringent eye exams, other various physical screenings, and intelligence tests. "I passed OK," grinned Eddie. The aviation cadets were a bit surprised that airmen were expected to go through basic training. The process lasted for many grueling weeks, where cadets would march and do close quarter drills in formation. If anyone protested, drill instructors reminded them that they were, "in the Army first, aviation second."

Ground school training in aviation was rigorous, with daily coursework on aerodynamics, engine systems, instruments, navigation, aircraft performance dynamics, and weather. The long days were demanding, and more and more cadets washed out. Undaunted, Eddie eagerly pursued his studies so that he could begin the actual flight training sequence.

In order to receive a commission as an Army Air Corps Officer, cadets were required to complete an accelerated college curriculum. The War Department made arrangements with colleges across the country to facilitate this training. To fulfill the requirements, Eddie enrolled at Centenary College in Shreveport, Louisiana. This small, Methodist liberal arts college was the oldest of its kind west of the Mississippi river.

Centenary College, Shreveport, LA (above)
Rosary College, River Forest, IL (below)

Eddie longed for Shirley's familiar help as he struggled through challenging Math and English classes without her. In April of 1943, Shirley accompanied Eddie's parents and younger brother Tom on a three-day journey, traveling from Maywood, Illinois to visit. After a pleasant reunion with his family, Eddie was eager to have time alone with Shirley. That evening, he had his chance. Eddie nervously drove Shirley to the Centenary College football field. With shaky fingers, he wrestled a ring from his pocket... as he asked for her hand in marriage, a police officer, flashlight in hand, approached them, "Sir, you should know better than to be out here at night." Despite the startling interruption and to Eddie's great relief, Shirley ecstatically accepted the ring. Competition from David Hogan and the U.S. Navy was officially over.

Shortly afterwards they informed Eddie's overjoyed parents. Shirley was eager to get home and tell her parents as well, but first had to endure the three-day return trip on a noisy troop train back to Chicago. Upon hearing the news, Park cooled the celebratory mood by insisting that no formal marriage would occur until after the war was over and Eddie was home safe as a "whole man." Marguerite, though very supportive of the couple, reminded her daughter to stay focused on her college studies.

Not long after Shirley returned to Chicago, Eddie successfully completed his college coursework, providing him the necessary credentials for the Officer training program. He and his fellow cadets then headed for classification schools in San Antonio, Texas, where they would undergo aptitude testing for selection as a pilot, bombardier, or navigator. After several more weeks, Eddie was placed in the official pilot curriculum and sent to Jones Field in Bonham, Texas for basic flight training.

6 SHIRLEY LITTON AND COLLEGE TRAINING

Early1943, Rosary College
River Forest, Illinois

Shirley flourished at Rosary College and was awarded a renewal of her academic scholarship for the following year. She elected a curriculum to explore her many interests, especially library science and botany. Although still undecided on a major area of study, her instincts pointed her toward library science.

From the time she was a child, her grandparents and parents encouraged her to read. She fondly remembered many evenings at home when her mother and father sat quietly across from each other in the living room, each lost in their own book. Shirley too loved books, and her vivid imagination allowed her to travel to foreign places, walk in a forest in the early evening, or have an exciting adventure at sea while reading. She always found it interesting to discuss an author with fellow students at Rosary College.

Sister Mary Ellen, Shirley's botany professor and a published textbook author, had a classroom that overlooked the beautiful campus. One entire side of the room was all windows, a panorama of color and variety of all the flowers and plants that ringed the campus courtyard. An Indian summer earlier that year left a rich blend of green, red, yellow, and blue petals throughout the carefully tended gardens. Inside the classroom, an array of plants in shades of light and dark green provided the laboratory with a rich assortment of study samples.

Sister Mary Ellen was a demanding teacher, interested in challenging her classroom of women. They focused on grafting techniques, plant classification, and rigorous memorization of plant types. Sister Mary Ellen left no quarter for students who did not enjoy the rigor of botany as a scientific endeavor.

Despite Shirley's high school interest in botany, library science was clearly her preference. "Besides," remarked Shirley, "I know I can get a job with my library science training." Shirley Litton soon declared a major in library science at Rosary College and felt anxious to complete the prerequisites and get on to the real training.

Summer-Fall 1943
Jones Airfield, Bonham Texas
Aviation Cadet Class #214

Aviation Cadet Eddie Tyre and his class #214 began flight training in the Fairchild PT-19 Army Air Corps trainer. The aircraft was a low wing, fabric-covered, two-seat training plane, with a straight six-cylinder, inertial start engine. Complete with open cockpit and a wooden propeller, the PT-19 flew at speeds up to 120 miles per hour. A flight instructor sat in the rear seat of the aircraft and communicated with his student pilot by shouting into a tube between the two, as no radios were

Aviation Cadet, Eddie Tyre   Sept 19th, 1943: Eddie pens a playful letter to Shirley from flight school

The PT-19 Fairchild used by the USAAF during Primary Flight Training

available at this level of training. Both instructor and student wore parachutes during the flights for an added level of safety.

During the first phase of training, instructors covered takeoffs, landings, and basic flight maneuvers, with a typical student soloing after ten to twelve hours of logged flight time. Eddie logged his solo flight in eight hours.

He missed Shirley dearly and often wrote to tell her of his experiences in flight school.

Hi Darling,

You know what your boyfriend did today? He soloed! 25 minutes in the air by his lonesome and it sure was. That back seat sure looked empty. Madame "Lady Luck" was in it for a couple of minutes (thank

31

heaven!) I think my instructor's hair turned grey while he watched
me. I got the traditional soaking after it was all over. Boy was I wet,
they stood me on my head and put a hose in my pant leg, water was
shooting out of my ears. I really enjoyed the bath. I've got those big
shiny solo wings on my cap... from now on I solo every day. Gosh!

Gee I miss you, Darling, no fooling. After 7months you'd think I'd get
used to it, but it's just worse. I want to see you more than I did when I
first got in... if that's possible... and it is. Sorry I have to close... been
an exciting day!

Still Yours, Eddie XXXXX

P.S. I still love you, too... that's standard equipment with me now!!

September 21,1943
Air Forces Training Center
Bonham, Texas

Training a pilot to recover a stalled airplane is challenging. The
aircraft is typically slowed to a minimal maneuvering speed, and
then the nose of the plane is raised slowly to reach a "critical
angle of attack". At this point, most airplanes experience a
separation of smooth flowing air over the wings causing the
airplane to buffet for a short period of time, and then drop
abruptly, nose-first. The wings stall and no longer produce
enough lift to keep the airplane aloft. Every pilot learns the
techniques necessary to recover from this event. Eddie recalls
not being particularly afraid of this facet of his training because,
"I really didn't know what was happening. I just did what he
told me to do."

After 9 weeks of basic flight training, Eddie began to sense
what it might be like to be a "real" pilot. He could successfully
perform maneuvers to bank the plane, stall and recover, and
even execute spin recovery techniques. During one harrowing
event, after climbing to an altitude of 6,000 feet, his instructor

required thirteen full spin rotations before allowing Eddie to correct their course. "I didn't really like that, but I did it... he was trying to set some sort of a record I think."

The PT-19 had no nose wheel and was referred to as having a "tail dragger" design. It was prone to ground loops, a dangerous phenomenon where aerodynamic forces caused the advancing wing to rise, pushing the opposing wingtip to the ground. In severe cases, if the ground surface was soft, the inside wing would dig in and cause the aircraft to swing violently or even cartwheel. The one time Eddie ground-looped his plane, his instructor swiftly and violently slammed the flight control stick back and forth between Eddie's legs, "I remembered the correct procedure after that!"

Advanced Flight Training
Barksdale Field, Perrin, Texas

Advanced flight training sent Aviation Cadet Tyre on to Perrin, Texas, where he was introduced to "real airplanes". He moved up from fabric-covered trainer aircraft to the aluminum-skinned Vultee BT-13, complete with a 200-horse power radial engine, a closed cockpit, and radio. The cadets started their training at Barksdale Field by flying long cross-country flights with an instructor. The training grew progressively more intense: flights without instructors, trips of 150 miles on a single leg, instrument flying (navigation without using ground references), formation flying, and acrobatic maneuvers.

As flight training progressed, the war effort overseas became increasingly foreboding and actual combat deployment for Aviation Cadet Tyre loomed. Eddie and Shirley traded letters almost daily throughout this period in their relationship, conveying the loneliness, romance, and apprehension they each

The Vultee BT-13 was the basic trainer flown by most American pilots during World War II. It had a more powerful engine and was faster and heavier than the primary trainer. It did not, however, have retractable landing gear nor a hydraulic system. The flaps were operated by a crank-and-cable system. It was nicknamed it the "Vultee Vibrator.".

felt. Excerpts from the letters, kept intact over the years, tell of the young couple's growing love for each other as they shared details of their lives.

Sheppard Field, Wichita Falls, Texas
Wednesday, March 13 1943

Liz Darlin,

I've just gotten back from the experience of a lifetime. I'll start from the beginning and go thru 'til the finish... please sit down... thank you. Monday morning at 4:00AM we were rudely awakened by the fireguard. We dressed and went to breakfast. Little did we know that would be our last decent meal for 3 days. Then we came back to the barracks and I got my bedroll and cartridge belt, gas mask, and knapsack. I went to the orderly room at 6:30AM and at 6:45AM we started our march... it lasted until 11:00AM.

It was only 15 miles. It didn't seem like that, more like 25! We set up tents... you should have been there... of all the butter fingers, at 2:00PM they were up?? From 12 'till 1 we ate. Now I know why they call it "mess." Among your issued equipment is a mess kit and canteen. We were told to clean our kits before eating. I did, with steel wool and soap. It didn't work as well 'cause when I got out there ready to eat the aluminum turned black! So I cleaned it again, most of it. I'll bet a dollar you wouldn't eat off it tho. After dinner you clean your mess kit and dry it and put it away. Then instead of resting after the morning walk we were assigned to work detail. Myself and 4 fellows were told to police the area around the river bank. We did, by lying down in the sun and resting. We were lucky that day. Then came evening mess... ugh... let's forget it... after dinner? We went on work detail again, but they only lasted 10 minutes when they called us together and gave us the fundamentals of the type of guard duty we were going to do that nite.

5 shifts, 2 hours each... Number 1 starting at 8:00PM. I had shift 2 to go on with the guard, it was good. I stood guard Monday nite and honest, from 10 to 12:45AM I never thought of you more than I have in my whole life. You kept me warm and it was cold. You'd be surprised how much thinking of a person will keep you warm. Nobody else could keep me warm just thinking of them! I never missed you more than I did those three days... whenever I got real cold I would think of you harder. It works!

Tuesday we went to the ranges. I shot a Thompson submachine gun... told where to hit a fellow to kill him and where to hit him to wound him... as if you had time to choose. Then we shot army rifles. It was fun, but I'd hate to be in front of them. In fact, it hurt enough just to shoot them!

Mind if I quit? I have to write Mother. I missed you all the while, darling.

Your soldier boy, Eddie XXXXXXX

A letter from Shirley to Eddie:

Rosary College
April 1944

Eddie Darlin',

The mailman just came and left 3 letters for Liz. One is from one of the gals at school, one is a catalog and general info from the U.S. Cadet Nurse Corps... in which I am interested. It all sounds pretty good. I have just about decided not to go back to Rosary College next fall, to go back to Halsey-Stuart for the summer anyway... and try to get into the Nurse aide work at night during the summer.

I won't be having any of that rare five-letter word anyway... DATES. So I might as well use up my evenings. I figure if I can stomach that type of work, I can probably stomach regular nursing. Lillian's sister Eleanor is going into the Cadet Nurse Corps in September, and is very enthusiastic about it. She did nurse's aide last summer and said it was wonderful. Also said you get plenty of dirty jobs... and some of the nice ones. She scrubbed floors, cleaned up patient's rooms, carried breakfast trays in and then out, also learned what the bedpan is for. She said she had the most fun when assigned to the maternity ward and men's floor. She said they make lousy patients, whine and fuss just like 'lil kids! Tell me what you think... The third letter was from the "Looey" (Lt.) I was sorry to hear that you might be leaving Shreveport. It sounds like such a lovely place and your friends are there, too! Where is Lake Charles? I cannot seem to locate it on the map.

Please write and tell me all about the "MARAUDER" I want to know... the news reports yesterday mentioned the Marauder in action over Italy. It seems to me that I've seen pictures of it and it looks somethin' like this: Remember I'm no artist...[pencil sketch omitted] I wish you could see the roses now. I've never seen such bee-utiful flowers. They have opened to full bloom, and they are absolutely gorgeous.

I thought your remarks about your brother using "our car"... well they were very sweet words. You ought to know that I don't mind them (Jack, too) using the car. They're both swell kids... we're lucky, both of us, having such nice families. And they are both such crazy people that they stay young! That's why I often ask you if we'll stay young and crazy too! We can be serious, too, for which I am grateful. After all, a gal looks to her guy for protection, and for a certain amount of masculine assertion! Not too much, though, 'cause after all... it's 50/50!!

We haven't any school today or tomorrow, so I'm taking advantage of the holiday. Mom, Jack and I are going to Evanston today to see Uncle Ben. I guess I better stop for now... I miss you and I love you, too! Your letter made me cry when you said, "I'd like to take you to Mass, too, but the 800 miles bothers me." Jeepers!!

God Bless you Eddie and Fly with you always, Love Liz

---

7 THE EVIL WORSENS

December 7th, 1943
Stalingrad Campaign, Russian Front

The German 6th Army, comprised of 300,000 troops and 2,000 Panzer Tanks, had been fighting the battle for Stalingrad since the summer of 1942. As the notoriously bitter winter of 1943 approached, the Red Army launched Operation Uranus, a two-pronged attack targeting the forces protecting the German 6th Army's flanks. Russian success ultimately cut off and surrounded the 6th Army in Stalingrad. Despite a lack of adequate supplies, Hitler ordered his army to stay in Stalingrad and make no attempt to break out: instead, attempts were made to supply the army by air and to break through the encirclement from the outside. By the beginning of February, the German 6th Army's ammunition and food was exhausted and they had no choice but to surrender.

This horrific battle lasted a total of 5 months, 1 week, and 3 days. To date, the Battle of Stalingrad remains the single bloodiest battle in the history of warfare. The casualty count from the Axis and Allied forces combined yielded 1.7 to 2 million men dead. The battle marked a crucial turning point in the European theater; the Germans never regained their advantage on the eastern front and, considering their staggering losses, were forced to pull forces from the west to fortify their positions throughout Europe[8].

Jewish prisoners with Nazi guards

During the era of the Holocaust, the American press did not always publicize reports of Nazi atrocities with prominent placement but in December of 1942, the *New York Times* printed the Allied statement condemning the mass murder of European Jews on its front page. Although the horrors of the concentration camps were not known until prisoners were liberated at the end of the war, the aviation cadets knew that Jews were being rounded up and deported from all over Central and Western Europe to their likely demise. The shared sentiment among Eddie and his fellow cadets was that Hitler and his Nazi party were truly evil and had to be stopped.

Spring 1943
Rosary College
River Forest, Illinois

Shirley completed the first half of her freshman year with continued academic success. With her renewed scholarship, she refocused her efforts on Library Science. Shirley received letters from Eddie several times each week, but there was noticeable change in his tone and subject matter. He often wrote about a desire to stop Hitler's progress in Europe, and shared with her his thoughts about impending combat. In his letters, Eddie looked forward to receiving his commission as a 2nd Lieutenant, and his aviator wings. He was excited to select the type of aircraft he would train with and ultimately fly in overseas combat.

They were both looking forward to the formal commissioning ceremony, but urgent need to train the cadets for overseas combat interfered. Fortunately, the cadets were granted a 30-day leave, allowing the newly commissioned 2nd Lt. Eddie Tyre a visit home. While on leave, Shirley, Eddie, and his family arranged a trip to Petit Lake. Relaxing during this break, the couple had a chance to discuss post-war plans and possible wedding arrangements. Eddie appreciated her parents' preference for delaying the wedding until the war was over. Meanwhile, Shirley thought of how she could save money and if continuing her studies at Rosary College made sense. Together, they discussed the differences in their religious backgrounds; Catholics frowned upon marriage between a practicing member of the Church and someone of an alternate

Eddie and Shirley enjoy a 30-day leave following the victory in Europe.

faith. These circumstances inclined the couple to consider Eddie's possible conversion to Catholicism.

The couple cherished their quiet time, talking in person about their future lives together after the war. Before long, Eddie's leave was over and he returned to combat training in Texas.

Spring 1944
Occupied France
Throughout the Country

The French were constantly aware of the German presence in France. Uniformed soldiers concentrated near transportation centers, government buildings, and airports. In both large and small cities, villages and towns, the Nazi flag and the uniformed German army were visible. The French people suffered terribly. They were resentful and afraid of the occupying power. Every day they felt the impact of the armistice signed in late June 1940 with the Germans. Designated as a military zone by the occupying force, the entire Atlantic coastline was off limits to French citizens unless they carried a special permission card. Critical shortages of gasoline, oil, and food debilitated the populace. French farmers were required to produce quotas of certain agricultural products, 20-30% of which were confiscated by the Germans.

Serious malnutrition affected children and the elderly throughout the country. Young French men were arbitrarily sent to Germany to work in forced labor camps to support the German war production effort. The free French press was taken over by Nazi propaganda programs. Gestapo and SS forces routinely searched out and murdered dissenters and supporters of the French resistance. All French citizens of Jewish ancestry, including business leaders, teachers, professionals, students, mothers, children, and the elderly were required to wear identification patches on their clothing when in public. Once identified, they were systematically rounded up, arrested, stripped of their possessions, and deported to "work camps" throughout Germany.

Rounding up French citizens

The Allies did not realize the full extent of the genocidal Holocaust until the end of the war. American and British liberators were horrified by their grisly discoveries at the concentration camps: in France alone, 800,000 Jews were killed, second only to the tragedy at Auschwitz, where over 1 million Jews were murdered. Throughout Europe, the Nazi program of mass extermination of the Jews killed nearly 6 million human beings.

Photographs this section courtesy of: (a) National Museum of USAF, (b) National Archives, (c) Tyre family archives

---

8 Darman, Peter, World War II "STATS-FACTS" (2007)

8 THE B-26 MARAUDER

April 1944
Advanced Flight and Combat School
Barksdale Airfield, Lubbock, Texas

> *"My first look at the B-26 Marauder... I fell in love with the airplane."*
>
> *2nd Lieutenant Ed Tyre*

The ship was sleek with powerful twin radial engines able to produce 2,000-horsepower each. Fitted with nose, waist, top turret, and tail guns (some of which were electrically driven), it was the fastest medium-weight bomber produced to date by the U.S. war effort. It was a lethal weapon. In the original design requirements, short wings were utilized to increase both speed and maneuverability at both low altitude and cruising altitude. The short wings also made it a more dangerous airplane to fly, due to instability at lower speeds, especially in the landings.

The B-26 Martin Marauder weighed over 25,000 pounds, carried a bomb load of 3,000 pounds, and had top speeds in excess of 285 miles per hour enabling it to keep up with many of the fighter escorts assigned to protect it. With a range of approximately 1,100 miles on full tanks, the Marauder was a formidable war machine.

The aircraft was entered from underneath the nose by pulling crew-members upwards into the forward section of the ship. This maneuver required strength sufficient enough to do a pull-up, but with the added weight of flight suits, parachutes, and flying boots, it was challenging to many airmen. The cockpit

area was small but allowed for both a pilot and co-pilot. Dual control systems were available if one of the pilots was injured during flight. A pilot-controlled 12.7-millimeter nose gun was available, but rarely used; the bombardier would move through the cockpit as the plane approached a designated target to operate the famous "Norden" gun sight and release bomb loads.

The B-26 Marauder had a service ceiling of 19,000 feet. Because it did not carry supplemental oxygen, cruising and bombing flight levels were restricted to a range of 8,000 to

The cockpit of the B-26 Marauder

B26 Marauders shown during formation assembly

10,000 feet, where oxygen was not required. This altitude restriction would cost lives, especially in raids through the Italian Alps. German anti-aircraft gunners quickly learned to manipulate this limitation by creating FLAK walls up to 12,000 feet, forcing the B-26 crews to fly directly into the line of fire.

In the spring of 1944, Army Air Corps 2nd Lt. Eddie Tyre began training in the B-26 Marauder. He soon met the crew he would stay with throughout the next 100 hours of flight: 2nd Lt. Jack Sorrelle, pilot, 2nd Lt. "Buck" Rogers, bombardier and navigator, Sgt. Wills, crew chief, Corporal Anderson, radio operator and gunner, and Corporal Wals, waist gunner and armament specialist. Over the next four months, the six-man crew flew formation training and perfected the technique with tighter and tighter maneuvers. They practiced simulated lost engine landings and drilled on recovery procedures. During bombing practice, they discharged 100-pound bombs from 10,000 feet targeting small circles on the ground below, honing

L TO R - LT. SORRELLE (PILOT) LT. TYRE (CO-PILOT).
LT. RODGERS (BOMB-NAV.) SGT. WILLS (ENG-GUNNER)
CPL. ANDERSON (RADIO-GUNNER) CPL. WALLS (ARM-GUNNER)
(331 AAF 61749) (1 AUG. 1944) BARKSDALE FIELD, LA.

the challenging technique over time. Eddie described his first impressions of flying the B-26 as "scary, the plane was so big, and the engines so powerful... I was used to a 200 horsepower single-engine airplane, the B-26 had two 2,000 horsepower radial engines!"

The airplane occasionally encountered a problem with "runaway props", which would place the propeller blades in flat pitch blade angle. This caused over speeding and possible disintegration of the propeller. Runaway propellers were especially frightening for aircrews due to their terrifying sound and the associated risk to the plane and crew. To avoid a crash on takeoff or landing in this scenario, the crew needed a long enough runway to shut the engines down and drain off aircraft speed. Fortunately, Barksdale Airbase had the longest runway available to the Army Air Corps at the time, measuring 10,000 feet. Army Air Corps engineers later made design changes to resolve the runaway propeller problem, modifying the battery system to allow pilots more reliable control of the propeller blade angles.

The B-26 was a controversial aircraft; so many young pilots were killed during the training sequence for the airplane that it earned the nickname "The Widowmaker". For a brief period of time, it was scheduled for cancellation until reputable aviator James Doolittle demonstrated that the plane was safely flyable if proper speeds were maintained in selected flight configurations. In response, the Army Air Corps adjusted pilot training procedures and made modifications to the wing design, but despite these changes, the B-26 remained a very challenging plane to fly. 2nd Lt. Eddie Tyre and his crew expertly overcame the difficulties with the airplane and successfully completed B-26 training. After a 5-day leave to Washington, D.C., he was ready for deployment overseas.

Photographs this section courtesy of: (a) National Museum of USAF, (b) National Archives, (c) Tyre family archives

---

9 THE WAR WIDENS

January 1944
Naples, Italy

In August of 1943, the Allies turned their attention to the
mainland of Italy, considered the "soft under-belly" of the Axis
Powers in Europe. Following the capture of Sicily by joint
British and U.S. Forces, the invasion of Anzio, Italy began on
January 22nd, 1944. Rains, mud, and a formidable German
counter-attack complicated the amphibious landings at the
Anzio beachhead. Hitler had earlier concluded that his Italian
Axis partner was weak and undisciplined, and had protected his
southern flanks accordingly. The Wehrmacht was firmly
entrenched in Anzio and throughout Italy.

The German presence in the Po Valley of the Northern Italian
Alps was an especially deadly force against the Allied raids flying
up the valley to attack railheads and supply bridges. Ground
forces, armed with anti aircraft canons, or
Flugzeugabwehrkanone (shortened to "FLAK"), fired 15 to 20
rounds of 88 millimeter shells per minute, with an effective
range of over 16,000 yards. On explosion, the shells would

German 88

scatter white hot metal fragments over an area of 200 feet. They easily pierced the aluminum skins of the B-26 and then penetrated vital internal aircraft systems, hydraulic lines, engines, propellers, and of course, the flight crew members. Germans used this capability to exploit the non-pressurized altitude limitations of the B-26 Marauders by creating deadly FLAK walls the crews were forced to fly directly through at 8,000 to 10,000 feet.

Deadly FLAK damage

Early Spring 1944
South Pacific

The Japanese considered the Solomon Islands and the Island of Rabaul as keys to the protection of the Japanese home islands. The Imperial Japanese Army was now regarded as a formidable enemy by the U.S. and the British. Japanese soldiers viewed death in battle as the ultimate opportunity for both personal honor and as a sacrifice to the Emperor. Surrender was not considered an option; to lose face by surrender was abhorrent to the Japanese military.

Their bloody battle for Tarawa won, a column of U.S. Marines marches to a pier.

Fighting throughout the Pacific islands was horrendous.

American losses were so high that the war department delayed reporting casualty counts after battles to manage public opinion and morale at home. Disturbing photographs of the dead bodies of U.S. Marines and Army soldiers littered along the beaches at places such as Tarawa, Guadalcanal, and Iwo Jima were not frequently published in the States. Even so, the public knew of the grave impact of these battles[9].

Many fighter planes and medium bombers, such as the B-26 Marauder, shared ground support to combat personnel as their primary mission. Following the eventual Normandy Invasion and victory in Europe, the U.S. Army Air Corps provided key strategic and tactical components in the defeat of the Japanese, and Eddie would potentially play a part in this.

Spring 1944
Elmwood Park, Illinois

Shirley spent her Sunday morning after Mass at St. Celestine's Church having breakfast with her parents. The American service member's flag hung proudly on the front door. The same distinctive white, red trimmed ensign with blue star was also displayed at Eddie's boyhood home in Maywood. This particular Sunday morning, their conversation turned to details about her boyfriend

Eddie and concern for her brother Jack, currently serving stateside in the U.S. Army Finance command in Pennsylvania. Everyone shared an intense interest in recent war news, especially given the slowly increasing record of Allied successes in both Europe and the Pacific.

At the Battle of Midway in 1942, carrier-based aircraft of the U.S. Pacific Fleet delivered a decisive blow to the Japanese Navy, sinking 4 Japanese carriers and a heavy cruiser. Over 270 Japanese aircraft were lost and 3,500 personnel killed. The battle was even more significant for the lack of U.S. losses; by comparison, only 1 carrier and 147 aircraft were downed. Guadalcanal Island, secured by U.S. Marines in early February of 1943, was yet another decisive victory for the Allies. It represented a land victory by the Americans against the Japanese, and provided a critical gateway base to the Solomon Island chain in the Pacific. With the additional success of Patton's Army in Sicily, Mussolini was removed from power, and shipping lanes in the Mediterranean reopened. The defeat of this key Axis ally served as proof that the Americans were a potent and growing force against the Germans and Japanese.

Park Litton (Shirley's father) was a very enthusiastic supporter of the American war effort - once he got beyond Roosevelt's maneuvering to "get us in." He commented on the importance of the steady successes and the effect on morale at home. Park was a combat veteran of World War I and understood the importance of support from home on troop morale. As a member of the 149th Artillery, 33rd Division, Machine Gun Battalion, he had seen vicious action in the French Argonne campaign, lasting 42 days, and personally experienced the horror of gas warfare in the trenches near Verdun. Park knew all too well the grizzly features of combat and its effect on men.

World War I Argonne campaign

Himself a victim of German mustard gas bombs, he suffered from damaged lungs carried home from the war.

Photographs this section courtesy of: (a) National Museum of USAF, (b) National Archives, (c) Tyre family archives

9 Darman, Peter, World War II STATS-FACTS (2007)

10 OVERSEAS COMBAT DEPLOYMENT

September 1944
Hunter Army Air Corps Field
Savannah, Georgia

2nd Lieutenants Eddie Tyre and Jack Sorrelle, along with their aircrews, picked up brand new B-26 Marauders at Hunter Field in Savannah, Georgia. In addition to the aircraft, they were also given new flight suits, parachutes, and .45 caliber pistols. Being issued personal weapons was a new and sobering experience for the young aviators, and Eddie later remarked, "For some reason, this made it all very real. I hoped I didn't have to use the thing." With their new equipment secured, the young pilots eagerly anticipated their 21-day journey across the Atlantic to the island of Corsica. This would mark Eddie's entry into combat operations in the Mediterranean.

After takeoff, anxious to know where they were going, Eddie and Jack disobeyed orders and promptly broke open the sealed orders that were issued to them earlier that morning. Their flight plan directed them south to Puerto Rico and then on to Natal, Brazil where they would wait for favorable westerly winds. From there, they would make the trip all the way to Ascension Island, located halfway between South America and Africa, off the North African Coast. Ascension Island, a British-held refueling and communications asset,

was approximately 34 square miles in area, roughly the size of the city of Washington, D.C.

Mountainous and volcanic, with a very short runway, this challenge was the first of many for the young pilots. The cruising range of the B-26 was approximately 1,100 nautical miles, so Eddie and Jack carried supplemental fuel bladders aboard to extend their range by an additional 500 miles. The flight distance from Natal to Ascension Island was approximately 1,400 miles. There was little margin for error, as no alternative airfields were available in the open Atlantic.

In contrast to an uneventful trip south from Puerto Rico, pre-departure flight briefings at Natal warned the crews of German submarines off Ascension Island transmitting false navigation signals to any aircraft flying overhead. If the crew picked up a false signal and flew off course, they ran the risk of depleting their fuel supplies, causing them to ditch in the open sea.

The next leg took them from Ascension Island to Liberia, West Africa, then on to French colonial Dakar, then Marrakech, Morocco, and finally Tunis on the North African coast. Despite the dangers, the crews successfully made the lengthy trip over the open Atlantic. After aircraft refueling and maintenance, the pair took off on the final leg to Naples, Italy where the aircraft was delivered and they were flown to their new command base on the island of Corsica in the Mediterranean Sea.

October 1944
432nd Squadron, 17th Bomb Group, 12th Air Force
Island of Corsica, Mediterranean

On arrival to the air base at Corsica, 2nd Lt. Eddie Tyre and the other arriving pilots were selected for combat crews. "It was a

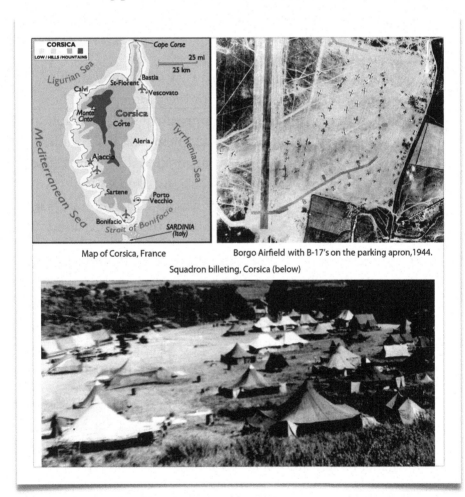

Map of Corsica, France   Borgo Airfield with B-17's on the parking apron,1944.

Squadron billeting, Corsica (below)

little like picking players for a baseball team... the Commanding Officer would walk along a line of pilots standing at attention and just say... you and you. Over there." The base housed twenty-four flight crews, six men to a team, selected from a pool of forty-eight pilots.

Ground crews maintained and repaired the eighteen available aircraft, quickly returning them to the flight line after each mission. Located along the beach near the port village of Bastia, the runway was necessarily short and covered with steel planking. During every takeoff and landing, crews confronted a harbor filled with the wreckage of Allied ships sunk by the Germans in an effort to prevent re-supply to their location.

Accommodations for the aircrews on Corsica were primitive. Tents, dehydrated food, and persistent bad weather made living conditions difficult for the men. Mess hall access was under a leaking tent with no chairs to sit on. Together with constant worry, living conditions, "mud everywhere, I mean everywhere," and the difficult missions flown into northern Italy, Eddie qualified the Corsica tour as "the worst."

2nd Lt. Eddie Tyre flew a total of six combat missions from Corsica before the entire bomb group was re-deployed to Dijon, France. These harrowing raids introduced Eddie to combat in the European theater and they were among his most dangerous. The missions were directed at the destruction of German railroad supply lines in Northern Italy, and took the aircrews over Milan and then through the Brenner Pass into the Alps. German anti-aircraft guns, placed strategically throughout the mountains, made damage during each raid unavoidable. The crews worried about FLAK risks on every flight.

"On my first mission, the FLAK explosions were interesting to see until we got into it. Then the FLAK was terrifying. It came right through the plane." Eddie piloted his B-26 into deadly conditions, while German air defense guns shot FLAK all around the plane. "We counted holes all over the airplanes after every mission. In fact, the worst of my missions, number six, we took FLAK right through the propeller, near the propeller hub – the hole large enough for my fist to pass through. How the propeller did not break off and come through the cockpit is unbelievable... just luck I guess."

The crews were not out of danger even while back at base. Eddie and the other new pilots were invited to watch a flight of B-26 Marauders return from a raid in Northern Italy. As the 3rd plane made its approach to land, a bomb accidentally released from the bomb bay where it had become stuck. Upon landing, the entire plane blew apart in front of the horrified pilots. All six crew members were killed. "Welcome to combat flying, gentlemen," remarked the Squadron Commander.

In another incident, 2nd Lt. Jack Sorrelle returned to base from his first mission with a plane so badly damaged from enemy fire that he was forced to make an emergency landing. With gear only partially down and locked, he crashed and the aircraft was

completely lost. Luckily, he survived this ordeal but it served as a sobering reminder of the ever-present danger the B-26 pilots encountered.

A Navy squadron of torpedo boats near Bastia launched night patrols into the Mediterranean, attempting to disrupt German and Italian supply ships headed for North Africa. Occasionally the Naval Officers from this squadron and Air Corps pilots on the base swapped personnel between missions. The practice ended abruptly when one Navy Officer, unfamiliar with base procedures, inadvertently walked into a spinning propeller on a B-26. 2nd Lt. Eddie Tyre, who watched this grisly event occur, reiterated his assessment that, "Corsica was the worst."

Photographs this section courtesy of: (a) National Museum of USAF, (b) National Archives, (c) Tyre family archives

11 CORSICA AND DIJON

October 1944
432nd Squadron, 17th Bomb Group, 12th Air Force
Dijon France

The 17th Bomb Group was re-deployed to Dijon, France in early November of 1944. The winter of 1944-45 was one of the most bitterly cold and unforgiving seasons on record in Europe. The aircrews were billeted in simple tents with no flooring, offering little defense against the cold. To deal with the lack of

available lumber, pilots transported wood planks on flights from Corsica to the new base in Dijon. Eddie and his buddies scrounged up a few extra planks and made a crude shack, providing a bit more warmth.

Previous to the Allies arrival, the Germans used the airfield at Dijon as a Luftwaffe base. Before abandoning the base, they destroyed most of the buildings and mined the runways. Allied crews removed the mines and repaired the runways by covering them with steel planks. The work was dangerous, not only because of the risk of triggering an explosion, but also because the small shrapnel pieces left on the runways could explode tires during takeoff. A 25,000 pound, fully bomb-loaded Marauder that lost a main gear tire on takeoff would crash and kill all aboard. Ground crews routinely lined up at an arm's length apart and walked the runways to remove such debris, but despite this, the risk remained and aircraft were lost.

Runway repairs at Dijon, France

December 1944
Dijon, France

In early winter, 2nd Lt. Eddie Tyre flew his first combat mission from Dijon, France to Neckargemünd, Germany to bomb railroad and marshaling yards. This raid was his first into German territory. The pilots were nervous about being shot down over hostile soil and many shared long-held fears of German invincibility. Briefings from the intelligence officers and rumors among aircrews added to the tension. Stories spread about enraged German citizens, angry that their cities were being bombed, capturing downed flyers and promptly hanging them.

Two full squadrons, 34 Marauders, were scheduled to fly with no fighter escort. During the three-hour ordeal on December 5th, Eddie and his crew encountered moderate levels of FLAK near and over the target, as well as on their return to base. No opposing German fighters were scrambled and no aircraft were lost. With this successful raid complete, Eddie's anxiety about flying missions over Germany was somewhat quieted.

Photographs this section courtesy of: (a) National Museum of USAF, (b) National Archives, (c) Tyre family archives

12 BACK HOME

Fall 1944
Elmwood Park, Illinois

Shirley Litton was conflicted over the right course to follow. She could either stay in college or leave school to find employment, saving money for the war's end and her upcoming marriage. Her parents, Park and Marguerite, were supportive and wisely counseled her that it was "her decision to make". For the time being, she elected to remain at Rosary College, although she felt growing unease over accepting renewed scholarship support.

She often stayed after classes to help in the war effort with many of her classmates. The Red Cross was sponsoring opportunities to roll bandages for the boys in service and Shirley not only participated several times but also helped to organize these events with her school. During this tedious work, the girls talked about their sweethearts in the service, thoughts on marriage, post-war plans, and troubling news from Europe. Like many of the girls, Shirley felt it was best to do her part and stay busy.

She had not heard from Eddie for what felt like ages and she wasn't sure where he was overseas. Shirley knew that the embarkation locations for European assignment were on the east coast. From what she pieced together from his previous sanitized letters, received from Hunter Field, Georgia, she surmised that he was in Europe rather than the South Pacific. Still, the nagging apprehension was there, "was he okay?" There was no way to know for sure unless Eddie's parents received the dreaded Western Union telegram. Park reassured Shirley during family dinners with his regular, up-to-date discussions of Allied progress in Europe.

To keep their minds off the uncertainties of the war, the Dominican sisters at Rosary College arranged for dates with young men from neighboring colleges who had not entered military service. But Shirley felt that "it just wasn't the same, everybody who had a fiancé or sweetheart overseas knew that."

Shirley had growing concerns for what the young couple would do for a living when the war ended. Eddie had shown great promise in his mathematics and architectural drawing classes at Proviso, designing two remarkable houses as part of his coursework. Shirley began encouraging Eddie to consider a career as an architect and even wrote to colleges known for their undergraduate architectural study programs.

Photographs this section courtesy of: (a) National Museum of USAF, (b) National Archives, (c) Tyre family archives

13 COMBAT MISSIONS

Winter 1944-45
432nd Squadron, 17th Bomb Group, 12th Air Force
Dijon, France

Favorable weather conditions allowed a series of raids into Germany through mid-December 1944, so missions were scheduled to take advantage of the clear visibility. On December 30th, 2nd Lt. Eddie Tyre and crew took off for a raid against the marshaling yards and troop barracks in Baden-Baden, Germany, located in a small, beautiful, mountainous region of Southern Germany near the Oos River. Surface elevation in the area was approximately 4,000 feet, allowing clear ground views by the airmen from 12,000 feet.

There were two squadrons with over thirty aircraft involved in this mission, and Eddie was in the second wave. The customary pattern for bomb runs included an immediate turn after the bombardier had toggled for "bombs away". As he banked the Marauder and deployed the bombs, it was the first time Eddie could see the full effect of the ordinance. "You could clearly see the buildings exploding. The mission took us over the targets around noon when the German soldiers were in the mess hall... it bothered me."

The remainder of the raid went well despite two brief encounters with some FLAK inbound to the target and outbound to the base in Dijon. The crews were spared any fighter opposition and returned safely to base, wrapping up mission number twelve for Eddie. He had only thirty-eight missions to go and then expected to be re-deployed to the South Pacific to deal with the Japanese.

HEADQUARTERS LIEUTENANT TYRE'S AIR FORCE

December 1944
Subject: A letter to his gal
To: His gal (naturally)

MaBelle Cherie' (someone told me it meant my beautiful darling)

My beautiful darling, I Love You!

Give you eleven guesses as to what I'm doing tonite. How dare you even think that- I never touch the stuff! Tonite I am what they call an Airdrome Officer. It's a detail given to officers that compares (favorably) to K.P. for enlisted men. The only halfway good thing about it is I get a jeep to tear around in. But they screw you there, cause you can't leave the operations room while on duty. Pardon me dear while I throw another log on the fire... pause... You know darling, we've just got to get a fireplace in our home. Let's get a home first, though. And getting MARRIED has the biggest priority of them all. Think you'll need any more than 25 hours? Hell I'll be ready in one. I don't know what's going to take you so long!!

By the way sis, the men all think your Dad's an on-the-ball character screaming for you to raise your dress higher. He must have been reading my mind. Hope he doesn't tell you everything he saw there. (France). Ouch don't slap me there.

Gosh darling, another Friday nite and no date with my one and only. We've sure got lots to do in the way of making up for lost time. That's one of the reasons I want to get married as soon as I get home so I won't waste 6 hours every nite from the time I take you home and pick you up the next morning. The biggest reason is that I LOVE

YOU so darn much I don't want to be away from you any more than I have to. You'll never really know how much I love you. They haven't got words that big!

Jeepers, did I pull a hell of a boner yesterday in town. I had just taken my first bath in 22 months and was standing outside waiting for "Mac" when my 6th, 7th, and 8th senses told me something was coming. Sure enough here comes a real cute girl down the street. So I says, "bon jour" in the sweetest French I could muster together. She smiled (so did I) and coyly said "Hello"!!! I quickly gathered myself from the sidewalk and followed her into the restaurant next door. I was giving her a very close going over (I can't help it darlin, all women fascinate me) when she starts talking fluent English to a guy I recognized as an actor in the U.S.O. show "Junior Miss". And then I recognized her. She was the star of the play, she was JUDY! At this point "Mac" came and got me which saved her from a dirty 2nd Lt.

Speaking of plays, "The Barrets of Wimpole Street" was a very good play. That Katey Cornell is O.K. for the number of years she has behind her. Brian Aherne can really pitch some ardent woo. I was all set to go to town today when the long arm of Capt. Miller (operations officer) reached out and grabbed me by the nape of the neck. He was very nice about it... asked me how I'd like the job of A/0 for today. So being an utterly truthful lad I told him I wouldn't. The curt reply was "T.S." I am now the A/0 for 24 hours. Only twelve more left, thank God. I am amazed at the neat letter I've written so far, and it's only taken me 21 and a half hours, too. Gosh, I'm tired darling. Didn't get to bed 'til 12 last nite on account of the play. Do you mind?

Good nite darlin 'X" I LOVE YOU Edward W. Tyre
2nd Lt. Air Corps
Airdrome Officer

14 TERROR WEAPONS

December 1944
London, England

The V-2 rocket had an effective range that made London and Antwerp, Belgium easy targets from Germany. War records establish that over 3,000 of the V-2 rockets were effectively launched into civilian targets. The *Vergeltungswaffe*, or "retribution weapon," was the world's first long-range, ballistic

missile. Unlike the earlier London Blitz weapons, which included bombers and later the "buzz-bombs," the V-2 was completely silent until impact. The rockets would leave a crater measuring approximately 60 feet in diameter with a typical depth of 20 feet or more. Records reflect approximately 9,000 civilian casualties from the weapons during their short usage at the end of the war in 1945. There were no effective counter measures to this class of *Wunderwaffe*, or "wonder weapon[10]".

Photographs this section courtesy of: (a) National Museum of USAF, (b) National Archives, (c) Tyre family archives

---

10 King et. al, "V-Weapons in World War II" (1998)

15 COMBAT MISSIONS CONTINUED

March 1945
432nd Squadron, 17th Bomb Group, 12th Air Force
Dijon, France

The raid planned for Neckargemünd, Germany on March 22nd, 1945, was a return trip for 2nd Lt. Eddie Tyre and his crew. Although previous B-26 bombing runs completely destroyed the rail yards, German slave labor had since rebuilt and they were once again operational. This mission included a full complement of thirty-six Marauders, with Eddie flying as first pilot (aircraft commander). They specifically targeted the bridge near the town center, and after releasing their bombs, visually confirmed bridge damage. The entire mission was peculiarly without incident; German fighters were sighted but they did not engage the bombers, and aircrews recorded no significant FLAK in their logbooks.

This unusual turn of events gave the pilots hope that the German war effort was wearing down. Back at base, there were rampant rumors of significant loss in Wehrmacht fuel supplies, and problems with spare parts for the Luftwaffe. 2nd Lt. Eddie Tyre logged his twenty-sixth combat mission, and his letters to Shirley began counting down the remaining missions left.

France
26 Missions
Liz Dearest,

I Love you... Things have quieted down to a dull roar. We're just sitting here shooting the bull. Got thru early with a small card game. I'm tired tonite as you would be, too, if you'd been where I've been. Most mornings when you're just opening your eyes... 10 to 1 says I'm over Germany.

"Peashooters" (fighter escorts) put on a show for us the last mission I was on. We called 'em up and asked for a little display. So they flipped 47's on their backs and circled the formation... did slow rolls around us... bunch of swell guys... sure made you feel good to see 'em sitting up there. Next time... it's fighters for me. But let's pray there's no next time.

Gosh darlin' there should be lots more for me to say. I guess I just can't get in the mood... please forgive me, but getting no mail for a while puts me in such moods. I love you darlin' and I'm getting less patient as the days go by. I want to get home... and married!!

Good nite dear,
"X" Love You
Eddie

April 14th, 1945
432nd Squadron, 17th Bomb Group, 12th Air Force
Dijon France

Eddie was in for a surprise on his thirty-fifth combat mission into Strasse, Germany. At the top of his crew manifest was a full U.S. Army Colonel and Division Commander. As Eddie recalls, "The guy was nuts to shoot all the guns aboard the plane... I told him politely that standard procedure required our B-26 Marauders not to fire our machine guns until after we had crossed over the Rhine river into German territory. He complied, but immediately upon crossing the river I could feel the waist guns firing, and then the tail guns going off. Then the top turret guns were being fired!"

In an effort to "manage" the Colonel's enthusiasm, Eddie invited him up to the cockpit to get a pilot's view of the trip back to base and final landing sequence. Eddie's next moments were unforgettable, "I made the most fantastic landing in a B-26 I ever made. I still don't know how I did it. I will never forget not even feeling the wheels touch down! He got out of our bomber and into a little J-4 Cub waiting for him at the airfield. He turned around and saluted me while I was still in the plane, and left for his job as a Division Commander... what a memory!"

When asked about a perfect landing, any pilot will be able to recollect at least one, maybe more. Often referred to as a "greased landing," aviators remember these events with great clarity. They require careful final approach speeds, exacting rudder control inputs to assure the tail section and fuselage are aligned correctly, and pulling the nose up at the precise moment necessary to create a partial stall, allowing the main gear to settle onto the runway without bouncing or skidding. Once this is achieved, slowly easing the control yoke allows the nose gear to gently come down onto the runway. This set of pilot-controlled maneuvers is a source of pride to aviators, usually unspoken, but surely remembered.

Spring 1945
Lechfeld, Germany

The Messerschmitt Me 262 Schwalbe was a revolutionary new Wunderwaffe. It was the world's first operational jet fighter. Able to develop speeds in excess of 550 miles per hour and heavily armed with four 30-millimeter cannons, the Me 262 was the ideal Luftwaffe weapon to be used against Allied bombers. The high-speed attack techniques used by the German Me 262 pilots were very difficult to defend against, as the Allied bombers had electric gun turrets, which were not fast enough to effectively track the jet fighters in aerial combat. In addition to cannons, the Me 262 fighters also had rockets with explosive warheads. A salvo of these rockets, fired out of range of the bomber's machine guns, repeatedly took down the famed, heavily armored B-17 Allied bomber, "The Flying Fortress". Allied pilots and war planners quickly determined that the only reliable method of dealing with these new German weapons was to attack them on the ground or during takeoffs and landings. The Luftwaffe countered with "FLAK alleys" of anti aircraft guns along the approach lines to protect the Me 262's on the ground[11].

On April 26th, 1945, 2nd Lt. Eddie Tyre and members of his crew along with an impressive "maximum effort" raid of seventy-four B-26 Marauders took off to attack the Me 262 primary base in Lechfeld, Germany. Eddie and his fellow airmen were nervous; they were well aware of the capabilities of the jets and the skilled German pilots who flew them. To bolster the effectiveness of this dangerous mission, a fighter escort of seventy P-47 fighters was attached to the squadron.

Messerschmitt ME 262 banking on the attack (above).
262's on the ground at their most vulnerable (below).

The pre-raid intelligence briefing warned that the Marauders were likely to encounter the jets eight to ten minutes before arrival at the target site. As predicted, the glint of the sun on jet cockpits was observed ten minutes from Lechfeld, putting the

Marauders on a raid over Germany

bomber crews on edge. On the first terrifying combat passes, the German jets destroyed nine B-26 Marauders and multiple P-47's. No Me 262 aircraft were damaged. From the cockpit, Eddie saw "an Me 262 flash under my left wing, and after a blink, it was gone. We had never seen anything that fast. It was very scary... In the flight of B-26 Marauders immediately behind our group, there was an immense explosion from a direct cannon hit to a Marauder. I watched Jack Sorrelle's plane lose control from the blast effect at 12,000 feet, only to recover at

2,000 feet. The flying skill was remarkable. I signed the form recommending Jack for the Distinguished Flying Cross! I thought he was done."

The first wave of bombers attacked the base at Lechfeld using a combination of 500-pound bombs designed to destroy the airfield's runways. A second, third, and fourth wave of bombers dropped smaller bombs, spreading charges horizontally to destroy the Me 262 aircraft on the ground. 2nd Lt. Eddie Tyre was a part of the 4th wave, successfully completing mission number forty-nine.

Photographs this section courtesy of: (a) National Museum of USAF, (b) National Archives, (c) Tyre family archives

---

11 Ethell, Jeffrey et. al, "World War II Fighting Jets" (1994)

16 HAUNTING MISSIONS

Late Spring 1945
432nd Squadron, 17th Bomb Group, 12th Air Force
Dijon, France

Eddie's very last combat mission in Europe would come to haunt him much later in life. The islands of Oléron and Royan, part of a small island grouping on the western Atlantic coast of France, were still occupied by German forces. The Allies had passed over the area in the push to reach Berlin after the Normandy Invasion. In coordination with French command, the Americans made a decision in the spring of 1945 in which Eddie and his 432nd squadron of B-26 Marauders would play a crucial role.

The pre-raid briefings for the pilots began in the usual bombed-out hangar just adjacent to the flight line at Dijon. Typical of most briefings, to ensure mission security, a large sheet covered the maps while aircrews assembled. When the sheet was removed, a map depicting the Atlantic coast of France was revealed. A long, black, felt cord stretched between Dijon and the target area. The Army Air Corps Intelligence Major explained the mission objective: liberate the French islands of Oléron and Royan from the Wehrmacht soldiers. He cautioned that the occupying forces were "thoroughly dug in."

The first wave of Marauders had dropped ordinance with blast effects that literally pulled the Germans out of their protective trenches and bunkers. 2nd Lt. Eddie Tyre and his aircrew flew in the third wave at a low level to deliver fragmentation bombs designed for anti-personnel effects. In a mission that lasted 4 hours and 40 minutes, it was the final few moments of the raid, that allowed the aircrews to see clearly German soldiers drawn out of their protective bunkers by the first wave of bombs. The impact of the first and second waves on ground troops was devastating. Eddie somberly remembers, "I could see the effects of our fragmentation bomblets. There was silence in the plane."

Photographs this section courtesy of: (a) National Museum of USAF,
(b) National Archives, (c) Tyre family archives

---

17 WAR IN THE PACIFIC

Late Spring 1945
Elmwood Park, Illinois

Shirley was worried about her Eddie. Despite the steady Allied move towards the Japanese home islands, the Pacific theater was proving a difficult and seemingly endless campaign. People at home were disturbed by the passion of their Japanese adversaries. Surrender was not seen as an option, and Japanese civilians were being equipped and encouraged to take up arms against the Allies.

Meanwhile, British and American war planners were preparing invasion plans for the Japanese main islands; the number of ships and personnel to be involved were staggering. No one knew anything about the secret "Manhattan Project" being readied for testing at Los Alamos in the southwest of the United States.

Hitler's suicide, along with his companion Eva Braun, announced the reality of a European war soon to be over. The Victory in Europe Day celebration at the Litton's home included the same group of friends that had gathered after the Pearl Harbor attacks. Conversation was upbeat, as young men from all over the community were heading home. Shirley learned of Eddie's orders to report to Santa Ana, California for a retraining program and possible deployment to the Pacific. She was relieved, at least, that the couple could be together again during his 30-day leave after all these months away. For Shirley, "it was like one world stopped and another was beginning. He was going to be coming home soon."

18 "EDDIE, YOU ARE ONE LUCKY BASTARD"

Spring-Summer 1945
432nd Squadron, 17th Bomb Group, 12th Air Force
Dijon, France

On the night of April 30th, 1945, the flight crew sergeant at Eddie's air base in Dijon ran through the tents and shacks shouting the news; Hitler was dead. As details confirming his suicide became available early the following day, crews throughout the billeting area broke out whiskey bottles and began drinking. Eddie and his flying buddy Jack drank until they were

EXTRA THE STARS AND STRIPES EXTRA

HITLER DEAD

Fuehrer Fell at CP, German Radio Says;
Doenitz at Helm, Vows War Will Continue

Churchill
Hints Peace
Is at Hand

dizzy and sick. The young pilots were not the only ones to raucously celebrate, firing their pistols into the air. Shortly thereafter, the Squadron Commander passed orders to collect the weapons so no one would get hurt.

Victory in Europe was officially declared on May 7th, 1945, and the squadron planned a victory flyover for the town of Dijon. The Commanding Officer gave 2nd Lt. Eddie Tyre the honor of flying the number two spot in the formation of seventeen Marauders, immediately to the right of the lead plane, flown by the Squadron Commander. On climb-out for the flyover, before they could settle into formation, Lt. Tyre and the crew heard a worrisome explosion, followed by another, and then another. The direction of the noise suggested a serious problem with the starboard engine. Eddie adjusted the throttle controls but the problem only worsened. Moments later, smoke and more explosions occurred almost simultaneously.

A lost engine in a high performance Marauder flown close to the ground is a life-threatening situation. The remaining operational engine has a tendency to "overcome" the lost engine side, leading to a disastrous loss of thrust. Simply put, the aircraft promptly loses its ability to climb. With sufficient altitude, a pilot can manage the situation with a controlled descent. The dead engine must be immediately shut down and the propeller "feathered" to avoid creating more drag and loss of speed. If an aircraft loses enough speed, the plane stalls and falls out of the sky. Unfortunately for Eddie and his crew, the victory flyover was planned to occur at 500 feet above the ground.

Eddie knew his airplane did not have enough altitude. He immediately ordered his co-pilot to shut down the erratic engine while fighting to keep altitude and avoid a stall. Declaring an emergency, he maneuvered the plane back to the airfield. All eyes were on 2nd Lt. Eddie Tyre as he successfully landed on one engine, sliding off into the grass and narrowly avoiding a tree, saving the lives of everyone on board. Eddie remembers that an ambulance and fire trucks were on the scene immediately, "They were waiting for us. When I exited the ship, my knees would not stop shaking."

The chief mechanic approached the airplane, "Well, lookee here..." One of the gasoline lines had worked itself away from the cylinder head and was spraying raw gas all over the engine. If the quick-thinking crew had not shut the engine down as swiftly as they did, the resulting explosion would certainly have taken the Marauder down with tragic loss of life. His buddy Jack, among those watching the event from the ground, commented, "Eddie, you are one lucky bastard!"

The drunken celebrations continued as the squadron of young pilots constructed an "Officer's Club" in the local chateau. Eddie, appointed as the club's "armament officer," arranged for a spare ball turret to be installed on the roof of the club. The revelers made trips to local markets in Dijon for additional supplies and liquor. However, their enthusiastic plans were foiled when the Squadron Commander got wind of their designs for the club.

As the partying subsided, aircrews turned their attention to post victory logistics. Eddie was assigned the job of ferrying B-26 Marauders to Antwerp, Belgium. Upon arrival at the airfield, he found neat rows of Marauders lined up for destruction. He recounts this heartbreaking event, "I remember being really sad at seeing these beautiful machines, which had performed so exceptionally well, being angled down into the ground after the nose gear had been cut off. I recognized tail numbers of planes

I had flown in combat in those lines of Marauders. I was sad..."

Back in Dijon, a list began to appear several times a week, detailing the names of pilots who were ready to be released home. A total of eighty "points" was necessary to qualify for the list: 2 points were awarded for each month of combat duty, 5 points for any air medal awards, and 5 points for participation in a major air battle. 2nd Lt. Eddie Tyre received 45 points for the nine air medals earned for bomb accuracy, another 20 points for his four major air battles, and enough additional points for each month of combat duty to make the list. His name appeared with orders to report to Le Havre, France and await a ship to New York. En route, he stopped in Paris, where he purchased a rosary for Shirley from the Cathedral at Notre Dame.

In July of 1945, Eddie began the 5-day journey back to America on board the USS Torrance, a fast cruise ship redesigned for troop transfer. As he boarded the ship, he exchanged his French francs for U.S. dollars. This gave him an immediate opportunity to play cards for money the entire way home, but he resisted the temptation, "I was smart enough not to play, I saw guys lose hundreds of dollars on the way home!"

Calm seas across the Atlantic made the trip home pleasant. Upon arrival in New York harbor, Eddie watched the New York City fireboats shooting sprays of water from their hoses high into the air to welcome the soldiers home. He remembers, "It was very moving to see the fireboats with the Statue of Liberty behind them. We were all happy to have made it through. There were crowds cheering and Red Cross girls with coffee for all of us."

On the train from New York to Fort Dix, New Jersey, each man was guaranteed a delicious meal. "The meals were great, and they served those steaks to us at 2:00AM in the morning, just like they promised!" From there he went on to Fort Sheridan in Chicago for a 30-day leave. Eddie's parents, with Shirley alongside them, met him there before Eddie was sent on to Santa Ana, California.

Photographs this section courtesy of: (a) National Museum of USAF,
(b) National Archives, (c) Tyre family archives

19 COMING HOME AND THE PACIFIC WAR THREAT

July 1945
Elmwood Park, Illinois

Revelers from all over Chicago were dancing and celebrating in the streets. The young couple ecstatically joined the festivities, happy, relieved, and ready to start a new life. They were eventually joined by some of Eddie's relatives for victory dinners all over town. It was a thrilling experience.

Eddie presented Shirley with the rosary, his gift

Courtesy of Wikimedia Commons
(Stars and Stripes - US-Army)

from Paris, "The rosary had great meaning to me, in fact I still have it to this day and I use it regularly." In anticipation of their wedding, Eddie took advantage of his 30-day leave to begin his conversion to Catholicism. He underwent formal catechism classes at St. Eulalia's Parish in Maywood, Illinois. One evening, the priest called Eddie's home to inform him of a scheduling change for class. His mother Pearl, unaware that her son had officially decided to convert, received the call. Her immediate negative reaction created strain for the young couple. One of Eddie's close friends, also in the Army Air Corps, and himself a practicing Catholic, encouraged Eddie to finish the process despite his mother's resistance. Eddie later remarked, "I'm very glad I did. It has been an important part of our lives together." As the couple looked forward, spring of 1946 seemed like an ideal time for a wedding.

Photographs this section courtesy of: (a) National Museum of USAF, (b) National Archives, (c) Tyre family archives

---

20 THE UNPLEASANT BUSINESS OF WAR PLANNING

The Pentagon, Washington, D.C.
Early Summer 1945

The young military officers finishing their duties in Europe were largely unaware of the grim affair they would face in the Pacific. Among them was newly promoted 1st Lt. Eddie Tyre, who had made his way to the west coast command and re-training program. Like most, he just wanted to get it all done with and begin his new life with his sweetheart.

In preparation for the invasion of Japan and its home islands, the United States manufactured 500,000 Purple Heart medals. Although macabre, the order was considered realistic given the topography of the Japanese mainland, the fanatic warrior codes of their military, and the anticipated use of the civilian population to oppose the Allies. Casualties for the ground forces were anticipated at over 1 million. "Operation Downfall" was split into two separate components; "Operation Olympic" was intended to capture the southern portions of Japan, while "Operation Coronet" focused on the Tokyo area[12].

Only a precious few individuals were aware of the Manhattan Project. Professor Leó Szilárd, a Hungarian-American physicist and inventor, was directly responsible for the creation of this clandestine program. In 1939, he drafted a confidential letter to Franklin D. Roosevelt warning of the Nazi development of nuclear weapons. He suggested that the United States develop its own such weapons and convinced his colleague, Professor Albert Einstein to sign his name to the letter in order to lend

Major General Leslie Groves and Physicist Oppenheimer discuss the results of the Trinity Test

Courtesy of Wikimedia Commons (U.S. Army Corps of Engineers)

credence to the proposal. The Manhattan Project would ultimately employ over 130,000 people with testing and manufacturing facilities throughout the United States. Its two primary goals were to develop a weapon that could provide enough destructive capacity to stop the war, and to gather intelligence on the German nuclear energy program. This program ultimately created the atom bomb.

On July 16th, 1945, at 5:29AM mountain time, the "Trinity Test" occurred in Alamogordo, New Mexico. This successful test firing of the world's first nuclear bomb demonstrated the

5:29am, July 17th, 1945, Alamogordo, New Mexico

Allied ability to develop, manufacture, and deploy a nuclear weapon. Later that day, a message was delivered to recently-elected U.S. President Harry S. Truman while he attended the Potsdam Conference with British Prime Minister Winston Churchill and Russian leader Joseph Stalin. The coded secure message read, "Operated this morning. Diagnosis not complete but results seem satisfactory and already exceeded expectations. Dr. Groves pleased."

Many of those involved in the Manhattan Project hoped that an additional bomb test, visible to the Japanese mainland, would demonstrate indomitable Allied power, giving them the opportunity to surrender and save lives. However, with the war weariness following events in Europe and the many casualties suffered in the Pacific theater, President Truman chose to use the atomic bombs destructively, over the protestations of Szilárd and other Manhattan Project scientists[13].

Hiroshima, August 6th, 1945

93

On August 6th, 1945, the first nuclear weapon ever used in wartime was dropped on the Japanese city of Hiroshima. Three days later on August 9th, 1945, a second device was dropped over Nagasaki. Shortly afterwards, the Japanese unconditionally surrendered.

World War II was over.

12 An excellent history of invasion planning for the Japanese home islands: Giangreo, Dennis "Hell to Pay: Operation Downfall and the Invasion of Japan 1945-1947" (2009)

13 A thorough review of the Manhattan Project is available in Rhodes, Richard "The Making of the Atomic Bomb" (1986)

21 NOW WHAT?

August 1945
Santa Ana Army Air Base
Los Angeles, California

1st Lt. Eddie Tyre traveled three full days to reach his new base assignment in California. His orders called for rest and relaxation and the Santa Ana Army Air Base was a perfect location for this to occur. Aside from the ideal weather, the attractions of nearby Hollywood and greater Los Angeles provided entertainment, restaurants, and shops of all kinds. Eddie was grateful to borrow his friend's car in order to visit Shirley's grandfather Roland Litton, who lived close to the base.

Military protocol required the personnel assigned to the air base to remain in uniform while recuperating from combat duty and awaiting new orders. Considering the immense pride that the American people felt towards their war heroes, Eddie's uniform created a stir wherever he went. After finishing dinner with relatives late one August evening, Eddie boarded the restaurant elevator to head home. The door opened and he was immediately greeted by a "giant of a man" with hands like "bear paws". Vigorously shaking Eddie's hands over and over, famous prizefighter Jack Dempsey exclaimed, "Proud to meet you, son!" before he joyfully exited the car. The elevator operator commented, "That Jack Dempsey is a great guy. He always tips, too!"

When news of Japan's surrender reached Santa Ana it was a welcome relief. But now what? What would the next steps be in Eddie's life? Remaining in the military was an option, of course, but the glut of pilots available after the war forced the Army Air Corps to downgrade the pay of any pilots wishing to stay on active duty to Master Sergeant (E6). This also meant the loss of officer status. "I was a 1st Lieutenant with 50 combat missions, it didn't seem right to me to be demoted!" Because of this predicament, Eddie made the decision to leave the military.

On October 17th, 1945, 1st Lt. Eddie Tyre signed his discharge papers. He was briefed on the pay and allowances due to him and officially transferred to the Inactive U.S. Air Force Reserve component. Soon after, Eddie returned home to his gal, Shirley, in Elmwood Park, Illinois. He managed to save almost $1,000 of military pay in a savings account, and now he was focused on a job and marriage.

Eddie arrived at Union Station in Chicago, Illinois to be greeted by Shirley and his parents, Pearl and Edward Sr. They were all filled with joyful tears upon seeing Eddie step off the train in uniform with a big duffel bag. They enjoyed a light dinner in Maywood before the couple set off to see Shirley's parents, where more tears and congratulations awaited them. Everyone was relieved for the safe return of the young airmen.

Along with thousands of other newly furloughed military pilots, Eddie was disappointed to find that the major airlines considered him too young for hire as a commercial pilot. "They told us at Eastern Airlines that the age cut-off was 26. I was only 21." Despite 50 combat missions and almost 700 flight hours, Eddie took a job at Eastern Airlines as a reservation agent. The position required a suit and tie, and a train ride to downtown Chicago every day of the week. After four months of this, he transferred to Midway Airport and was quickly promoted to a ticket agent. This position required a special uniform and more distant travel to the airfield each day. Eddie was frustrated with the 5-year wait list for a flying job, but was grateful to have gainful employment so he could focus on his future with Shirley.

In order to proceed with their marriage, Eddie needed to complete his conversion to Catholicism. Shirley's parents offered to be his godparents at his formal baptism, and he graciously accepted. Although Shirley and her parents attended the ceremony, the tension over this event remained for Eddie's parents and they did not attend the baptism.

With the constraints of his newly adopted Catholic faith, Eddie found the selection of a wedding date to be unusually tricky; the spring tradition of Lent required reflection and fasting, which would make a wedding celebration inappropriate during this time. Out of respect for the Catholic faith and Shirley's family, the couple chose March 2nd -- before the formal Lenten season -- to allow for, in Eddie's words, "a great party".

Next was the daunting task of preparing invitations. Eddie invited his Army Air Corps buddies to be groomsmen: Bob Bunting (pilot), Bob McMillan (bombardier), Chuck Bloomquist (bombardier), and Hugh Galston (pilot). Meanwhile, Shirley confirmed her list of bridesmaids and her matron of honor. Her cousin George Lindstrom, a Marine Corps aerial photographer during the war, would be the official wedding photographer.

The couple spent their time working and saving money in anticipation of their married life together. Eddie's combat pay and Shirley's earnings gave the couple a combined savings of about $1500. They enjoyed free time with other couples that had also returned from wartime service, reminiscing about various World War II events. Often, their evenings were filled with laughter, as the gals recounted their wartime activities in college, the Red Cross, or working to support the war effort, while the men humorously compared the benefits of one military branch over another with the playful camaraderie common among veterans.

As the wedding day approached, Eddie and Shirley both grew nervous about their "big day". The couple planned two separate ceremonies so that a Catholic mass could occur at 8:00AM, followed by a civil ceremony later the same day at 4:00PM. Proud that his military buddies would attend, and feeling that "tuxedos are too expensive," Eddie and his groomsmen intended to wear their military uniforms.

His parents and high school-aged brother Tom attended the civil ceremony. Pearl, still uncomfortable with Eddie's conversion to Catholicism, refused to allow the family to attend the Catholic mass. Eddie's brother Bob, stationed in Germany with the U.S. Army of Occupation, sent his congratulations from overseas.

"Stay calm… stay calm…" Shirley repeated to herself, as the traditional wedding music began to play. The crowd stood up and watched as Park Litton, smartly dressed in a tuxedo, walked his daughter down the aisle. Surrounded by family and friends, Shirley couldn't help but smile with every step. Standing at the

front of the church, as his bride approached, Eddie thought, "she just looked beautiful, just looked beautiful, I couldn't believe how beautiful she looked." At the end of the ceremony, the newly married couple clasped hands and walked outside to be greeted by a throng of guests throwing rice. Park had arranged for their "getaway" car, a 1939 dark blue Nash coupe, playfully decorated with tin cans tied to the bumper. The crowd cheered as the two drove away, cans rattling noisily behind them.

The couple hosted a festive celebration that evening at Anderson's, a restaurant in River Forest, where their guests enjoyed dinner and conversation, at one point cheering as Eddie fed his bride a bit of wedding cake. Shirley's father gave a speech, praising the newlyweds and playfully cautioning his new son-in-law, "Make sure you take care of my Scottie."

Their honeymoon took the couple to an intimate ski resort in Phelps, Wisconsin. During their five-day trip, Eddie and Shirley enjoyed cross-country skiing and quiet dinners, and being

Honeymoon in Phelps, Wisconsin with Park Litton's 1939 Nash

"treated like royalty by the small staff". Getting to Phelps meant a several hundred-mile drive into the northern part of Wisconsin, and they were happy to have each other during the blizzard that struck their return trip.

The end of the war saw the return of many service men eager to begin their new lives and start families. This set of circumstances created a shortage of available housing across the country. Back in Illinois, Shirley and Eddie began their frustrating search for a home of their own but were unsuccessful. Fortunately, Park Litton made good on his offer to remodel the attic space for them as a fallback option and fall back they did, living upstairs for the first five years of their marriage.

In 1955, Eddie transitioned to the active reserve component of the U.S. Air Force. He flew C-46 transport aircraft before moving on to the C-119 "Flying Box Car". By the time he retired, at the rank of Lt. Colonel, Eddie Tyre had completed 26 years of commissioned service.

Sixty-eight years later, at 91 years of age, Eddie and Shirley remain happily married with 7 children, 14 grandchildren and 7 great-grandchildren. They settled in southeast Wisconsin where they still enjoy close relationships with family. Their unwavering devotion to each other continues to this day.

22 THE MARTIN MARAUDER

The B-26 Martin Marauder failed to live up to its reputation as "The Widowmaker" for 1st Lt. Eddie Tyre. This challenging aircraft transitioned through design changes, then specialized pilot selection and training, to eventually become the U.S. Army Air Corps aircraft with the lowest combat loss rate of World War II. This has been attributed in part to engineering design changes, but more so to the extraordinary aircrews and pilots that flew the Marauder in over 110,000 documented combat sorties. The B26 Martin Marauder had a remarkable series of "firsts" for the Army Air Corps.

The B26 Marauder was the 1st Army Air Corps bomber to:

1) Deploy a torpedo

2) Complete 100 missions

3) Complete 200 missions

4) Complete 300 missions

5) Employ wide use of plastics in place of metal

6) Carry a bomb payload larger than the four engine B-17

7) Use flexible tracks to convey machine gum ammunition to turrets (thanks to the Lionel Trains manufacturing company)

8) Have an aerodynamically "perfect" fuselage

Of particular interest, the Martin Marauder B-26 plants produced 5,266 aircraft during the war, and at present there are only 4 complete planes left. The Pima Air and Space Museum in Tucson, Arizona is presently restoring a 5th Marauder and hosts a B-26 Marauder historical archive complete with a robust collection of records, photographs and a dedicated archivist helpful to this author in completion of this book.

23 THE FRENCH LEGION OF HONOR (CHEVALIER)

April 2013
Governor's Mansion, Madison, Wisconsin

Four generations of Tyre and Litton family members gathered from all over the United States at the Governor's mansion to celebrate a hero. In the ceremony to follow, Lt. Colonel Edward W. Tyre, USAF (ret), would officially be awarded the most prestigious medal and highest honor possible by the French government, The Legion of Honor, Chevalier.

In the year 1802, Napoléon Bonaparte commissioned the "Ordre national de la Légion d'honneur" as the highest decoration in France. The award is divided into five degrees, the highest of which is the *Chevalier*, or Knight. The medal is awarded for "excellent civil or military conduct delivered, upon official investigation". One of the more notable World War II recipients of the Legion of Honor medal is General Dwight D. Eisenhower, Supreme Allied Commander in Europe during that conflict.

Major General Donald P. Dunbar, USAF, the serving Adjutant General for the State of Wisconsin, began his speech honoring the Lt. Colonel Edward W. Tyre, USAF (ret) by discussing the meaning of freedom and the costs required to preserve it. He spoke of family traditions of service and the great contributions made by the young men and women who served this country during World War II, and the many conflicts since that time.

To officially convey the decree of French President François Hollande, the French Ambassador to the United States, Monsieur François Delattre appointed Lt. Colonel Edward W. Tyre to Chevalier of the French Legion of Honor.

Washington, D.C.
November 30, 2012

This award testifies to President Hollande's high esteem for your merits and accomplishments. In particular, it is a sign of France's infinite gratitude and appreciation for your personal and precious contribution to the United States' decisive role in the liberation of our country during World War II. The Legion of Honor was created by Napoléon in 1802 to acknowledge services rendered to France by persons of exceptional merit. The French people will never forget your courage and your devotion to the cause of freedom. It is a true pleasure for me to convey to you our sincere and warm congratulations.

Following an additional speech by U.S. Navy Captain Timothy Tyre (ret), expressing the pride of the family members gathered, an especially moving presentation was offered by Monsieur Alain Peyrot, Professor Emeritus from the University of Wisconsin, himself a child during the French occupation. He spoke about the impact of persecution by a foreign power. He recounted food shortages and fear of reprisal against family members and citizens who participated in the resistance. Throughout these heartfelt sentiments, he shared his personal

"Men like Lt. Col. Tyre - who comprise our greatest generation - answered the call and saved the world." — Maj. Gen. Dunbar

experience of losing one's freedom, and the subsequent gratitude the French people have for the American liberators. The Consulate General of France in Chicago Graham Paul then read the following:

Dear Colonel Tyre,

It is a great honor and privilege to present you with the Knight of the Legion of Honor medal. Through this award, the French Government pays tribute to the soldiers who did so much for France and Western Europe. More than 65 years ago, you gave your youth to France and the French people. Many of your fellow soldiers did not return, but they remain in our hearts.

Thanks to the courage of these soldiers, to our American Friends and Allies, France has been living in peace for the past 6 decades. They saved us and we will never forget. I want you to know that for us, the French People, they are heroes. Gratitude and remembrance are forever in our souls. You, Mr. Tyre, are among those heroes. You enlisted in March 1944 as a 1st Lieutenant in the 17th Bombardment Group of the 432nd Squadron. From October 1944 to July 1945 you participated in the Rome-Arno, Northern France, Rhineland, and Central Europe Campaigns.

For your achievements, the American Government presented you with prestigious awards including the Air Medal with eight Oak Leaf Clusters, the EAME Theatre Ribbon, and the Distinguished Unit badge.

To show our eternal gratitude, the Government of the French Republic has decided to award you the Legion of Honor. Created by Napoléon, it is the highest honor that France can bestow upon those who have achieved remarkable deeds for France. Thank you for what you did and congratulations.

"You wanted France to be free, and you fought to liberate its people. What higher deed exists than yours?" — Graham Paul

After the medal was bestowed upon him, and much to the delight of those present at the ceremony, Lt. Colonel Edward W. Tyre made a request to speak. His speech was short and reflective of his humble personality.

Thank you, merci beaucoup, la belle France,

Thank you, France, for making this event possible. Thank you, General Napoléon for creating this award in 1802. Thanks to Consul General Graham Paul for the honor he brings to this ceremony.

I am just sorry most of my comrades are gone, either lost in battles in France during the war, or age has taken its toll. I accept this award with humility and pride in all our names. The short ten months I spent on French soil at the airfield in Dijon during the war was very exciting to say the least, everlasting in my memory to say the most.

The winter of 1944-45 was one of the worst ever experienced in Europe and it was made worse by the war and its misery. But in spite of Nazi Germany and adverse weather we got the job done. Far too many soldiers, sailors, and airmen were left over there. But we did get the job done and most of us returned home. Let's hope that we who are still here learned a huge lesson; there are no winners in war and everyone is hurt in some way.

Again, I say to everyone in this room, thank you for coming, thanks to the Republic of France, and special thanks to the United States Air Force. A really special thanks to our oldest son, Captain Tim Tyre, and to all our other kids, Doug, Brian, Dr. Chris, Kevin, Meg, and Betsy for arranging this affair with lots of help from Adjutant General Dunbar's staff. Merci beaucoup to the Republic of France and Mr. Graham Paul, the Consul General, and especially to my charming bride of 67 years, Liz.

Early in our trip to Europe, courtesy of the United States Air Force, we flew six missions into Northern Italy, actually the Alps and the Brenner Pass, which was the only railroad connection to Nazi Germany. After bombing the railroad bridges and marshalling yards, we would exit Italy over Venice. No bombs could be dropped on

Eddie and Shirley, April 6th, 2013

Venice. We headed south down the Adriatic coast to the battle line across Italy, turning across and onto the Mediterranean headed for Corsica. In our trips back to Corsica we passed over the Island of Elba, where Napoléon was incarcerated for a time. Little did I realize that he had a big hand in designing the medal I received today in the year 1802. So I salute General Napoléon for creating this medal!

For myself and my comrades...thank you.

EPILOGUE

I wrote this book because I love and respect my parents. I wrote this book because my Dad has always been a hero to me. I grew up with small town values, in a post-World War II era. Families were large and I was blessed with parents who worked hard and encouraged all seven of their children in every possible way to achieve in school and sports.

Some of my earliest recollections include my Dad returning from U.S. Air Force missions in a flight suit and flight bag, grinning. He was and still is a humble man, who makes no special effort to draw attention to himself. As I grew older, the impact of what he did during World War II, and what my parents went through as a young engaged couple during those years, made me appreciate them more and more.

When I was commissioned in the U.S. Navy my parents were proud of me. As I came to understand what military service was really all about, the depth of my respect for what my Dad went through grew deeper. After completing civilian pilot training many years ago, my first passenger was my Dad. While I was busy attending to the aircraft, I glanced over to see him tearing up. It was a special moment. Later, I completed aviation ratings to allow me to teach ground school to young aviators. Often, I asked my students after weeks of complicated aviation related classroom material, if they had an interest in meeting a retired

World War II combat pilot. I never told them ahead of time who the guest speaker would be. I noticed during those visits to our flight classes, that my very quiet father became quite animated, and he related stories from the war years I had never heard. I gave some thought to writing a book about him, but the task was daunting and I was busy.

Immediately following the 911 attacks, I received a call from my Dad (he was 80 years old at the time). I was on duty at the Pentagon and was still recovering from the surreal events that surrounded that difficult day. His comments were brief... "Are you OK? ...This is your Pearl Harbor, you guys have to work this thing." His comments were classic Dad. Then I knew I had to write this book. When I finally started, I couldn't stop. I hope you enjoyed this special love story about "The Widowmaker".

CAPT Tim Tyre, USN (ret)

ABOUT THE AUTHOR

Timothy E. Tyre is a retired U.S. Naval Officer with 22 years of commissioned service and is the eldest of Lt. Colonel and Mrs. Edward Tyre's seven children. Tim and his wife Marilyn raised four children and are blessed with five grandchildren. He presently directs the Aviation Science programs at Carroll University and St. John's Northwestern  Military Academy. He teaches both private pilot and advanced instrument ground schools at Spring City Aviation in Waukesha, Wisconsin. An instrument-rated pilot, Tim appreciates the challenges and joy inherent to aviation. This is his first book.

Ready to go to War, 1944

APPENDIX I: LT COLONEL TYRE'S WWII UNIT INSIGNIAS

LT Colonel Edward Tyre's WWII Unit Insignias

432nd squadron

17th Bomb Group

12th Air Force

APPENDIX II: LT COLONEL TYRE'S WWII MISSIONS

31 Oct 1944................Nervessa
04 Nov 1944................Ala
05 Nov 1944................Pontetidine
08 Nov 1944................Peschiora
11 Nov 1944................Ora
16 Nov 1944................Rovereto
05 Dec 1944................Neckargemund
10 Dec 1944................Breisach
14 Dec 1944................Obr Otterbach
19 Dec 1944................Landau
23 Dec 1944................Neckargemund
30 Dec 1944................Oos
02 Jan 1945................Thaleischweiler
22 Jan 1945................Rastatt
29 Jan 1945................Wissembourg
02 Feb 1945................Offenberg
08 Feb 1945................Apenweier
19 Feb 1945................Lahr
22 Feb 1945................Nufringer
23 Feb 1945................Carlsberg
02 Mar 1945................Seigelsbach
13 Mar 1945................Kirchel
15 Mar 1945................Siegfried Line
16 Mar 1945................Siegfried Line
19 Mar 1945................Siegfried Line
22 Mar 1945................Nechargmund

23 Mar 1945................Heidelberg
24 Mar 1945................Kochendorf
31 Mar 1945................Heilbronn
02 Apr 1945................Boblinger
05 Apr 1945................Klein Engstinger
06 Apr 1945................Gailenhausen
10 Apr 1945................Schweinfurt
11 Apr 1945................Strass
14 Apr 1945................Strass
15 Apr 1945................Roube
16 Apr 1945................Jaffe
16 Apr 1945................Coubre
17 Apr 1945................Dettelslau
18 Apr 1945................Schussenreid
24 Apr 1945................Schwabmunchen
25 Apr 1945................Lechfele (Me262 Fighter Jets)
30 Apr 1945................Oleron Island

REFERENCES

Personal Interviews

1) Personal interviews with Lt. Colonel and Mrs Edward Tyre, USAF (ret)

2) Lt. Colonel Edward Tyre, USAF (ret); military records, WWII mission documents, photos and memorabilia.

3) Personal photographic collection, Lt. Colonel and Mrs Edward Tyre, USAF (ret)

4) Personal letters from a collection of original WWII era letters sent between Edward Tyre and Shirley Elizabeth Litton.

5) Consultation with Andrew Boehly, Curator of Collections and access to B-26 Marauder archival materials and photographs Pima Air and Space Museum, Tucson, Arizona. 2015

Reference Material

6) Agawa, Hiroyuki, The Reluctant Admiral: Yamamoto and the Imperial Navy, NY: Viking Press 1979

7) Churchill, Winston S., The Gathering Storm, Houghton Mifflin Company, 1948

8) Darman, Peter; World War II, Facts and Stats, Metro Books, New York, 2009

9) Ethell, Jeffrey and Alfred Price. World War II Fighting Jets. St.Paul MN: Motorbooks International, 1994

10) Giangreco, Dennis M. Hell to Pay: Operation Downfall and the Invasion of Japan 1945-1947, Annapolis, MD, Naval Institute Press, 2009

11) Johnson, David C. (1988), U.S. Army Air Forces Continental Airfield (ETO), D-Day to V-E Day, Research Division, USAF Historical Research Center, Maxwell AFB, Alabama

12) King, Benjamin and Timothy J. Kutta. Impact: The History of Germany's V-Weapons in World War II. Rockville Centre, NY: Sarpedon Publishers, 1998

13) Rhodes, Richard. The Making of the Atomic Bomb. NY Simon & Schuster 1986

14) Smith, J. Richard and Edward J. Creek. Jet Planes of the Third Reich. Boylston, Massachusetts: Monogram Aviation Publications, 1982

15) Smith, Peter C. The Junkers JU87 Stuka: A Complete History, London: Crecy Publishing Ltd. 2011

16) Speer, Albert et al., Inside the Third Reich: Memoirs. New York, Simon and Schuster, 1997

17) Weintraub, Stanley., Long Day's Journey into War, Lyons Press, 1991

External Links

1) The archive about the assignment of persons and material of the German Air Force in the Second World War (http://www.luftarchiv.del)

Made in the USA
Columbia, SC
04 February 2018